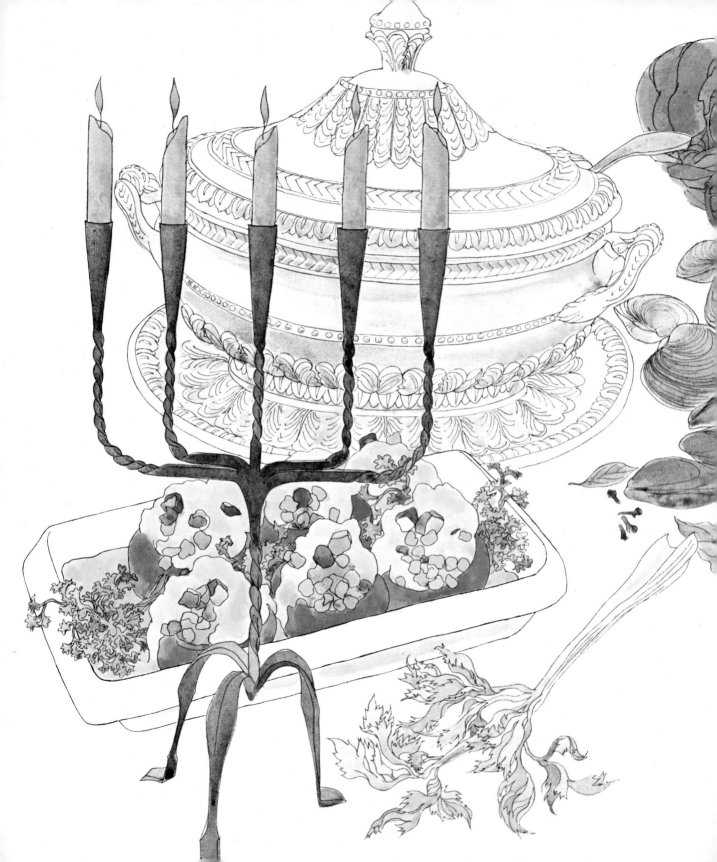

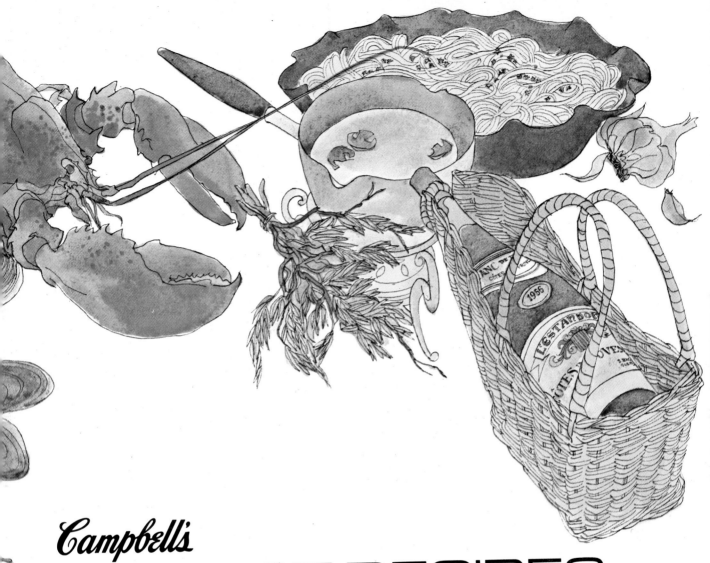

Campbell's 100 BEST RECIPES

Plus 157 Other Family Favorites and Party Dishes

Prepared and Tested by Home Economics Department
Campbell Soup Company

Photographer • Al Gommi
Artist • Joan Blume
Art Director • Gerard Nook
Contributing Editor • Kay Shaw Nelson

Dedication

This book is dedicated with much appreciation to American homemakers who enthusiastically seek new food ideas to offer their family and friends.

Carolyn Campbell

Home Economics Department

CONTENTS

INTRODUCTION

With fond memories of the past and enthusiasm for tomorrow's world of food, we present this new cookbook.

"Cooking with Campbell's" has long been a favorite byword among American homemakers who rely on a rewarding repertoire of high-quality convenience foods. Today there are many such foods, all designed to assist you in planning and serving quick and easy family meals, as well as elegant and economic repasts for entertaining.

We offer this treasury of recipes and entertaining innovations with our favorite motto:

"To make the best, begin with the best—then cook with extra care."

All of us love good food and like to dine well. But few have time to create complicated dishes which take hours of painstaking preparation.

Food is one of your prime concerns. As wife you "rule the roast" (at least until the master of the house moves the grill outdoors), as mother you care for the nourishment of the children. Of course, you are also shopper, always in the market for the budget-best. And as hostess you must provide gracious hospitality, keeping in mind the dictum of the famous French gastronome and writer, Brillat-Savarin, "To invite someone is to take charge of his happiness during the time he is under your roof."

Today, by taking advantage of convenience foods available in intriguing and abundant variety, you can quickly prepare fine meals for family and guests. With carefully tested recipes and good planning it is easy to become a connoisseur of food and to entertain with distinction.

That's what our book, "Campbell's 100 Best Recipes," is all about.

As our home economics staff was preparing for the 100th Anniversary of the Company, we reviewed our long experience in providing proven recipes and menus for American homemakers—as well as the response from many homemaker letters about their own favorites. It seemed timely now to pass along in one volume a collection of "100 Best Recipes" using condensed soups. The selection process was most difficult because of the great number of favorites in our test kitchen files. But we finally did choose the "100 Best Recipes"—while also including another 157 recipes equally appealing as the "100 Best."

This book combines popular recipes from the past and contemporary selections, many internationally inspired.

You will find enticing ideas for entertaining, including menus for such enjoyable occasions as gala luncheons, weekend brunches, patio parties, buffets, barbecues, informal dinners, and late evening get-togethers.

The tastes of all ages and the demands of a wide variety of mealtime situations have been kept in mind. There are superb Souper-Snacks for children, Souperburgers for teen-agers, casseroles for company, elegant entrees for luncheons, hearty dishes for men, savory selections for devotees of the outdoor barbecue, gastronomic creations for foreign food enthusiasts, and dining suggestions for the calorie-conscious crowd.

"The glory of the house is hospitality" were the words of an early American fireplace motto. For any event in the home, whether a children's after-school celebration or a handsome dinner party, the statement is still sound. The pride and pleasure of entertaining in the home is one of our greatest joys.

"Helps For the Hostess," published by the Joseph Campbell Company in 1916, advised the women of that day on how to give "a successful formal dinner" and "an informal dinner with one maid." Alas, that was yesteryear!

Today you have a diversity of convenience foods and the heritage of the world's eating treasures at your disposal. We hope this collection will assist you in enjoying them to the full, in entertaining successfully with economy and elegance, with fun and flair, and without help—but withal in a convivial atmosphere.

"We blend the best,
with careful pains
In skillful combination,
And every single can contains
Our business reputation."

Carolyn Campbell

The "100 Best Recipes" are marked with this symbol . . . ❋

APPETIZERS

A prime virtue of the appetizer is that its culinary role is well defined and easy to comprehend. These tasty tidbits, whether a few or a selection, are designed to enchant the eye, please the palate, and whet the appetite. The marvelous morsels may be canapes, spreads, dips, relishes or more elaborate hot combinations. Make them as pretty as possible, for as openers to any gastronomic get-together they set the scene; even if their appearance is brief, it is, nevertheless, extremely important.

Like so many of our culinary customs, the enjoyment of appetizers is anything but new. Ancient Greeks relished a few "provocatives to drinking," as they were then dubbed, with goblets of wine. The *gustatio*, or first course, of the Romans was an elaborate array of dishes of many kinds and tastes. In Europe it has long been customary to begin any repast with a glittering, taste-tempting appetizer assortment. In Russia there is the galaxy of *zakuski*. Scandinavia has its bountiful *smorgåsbord*. Italians are devotees of *antipasto*, and in France there are the heavenly hors d'oeuvres. Austrians and Germans adore their varied and inviting *vorseeisen*. In sunny Spain the pre-meal snacks, *tapas*, include an amazing selection of seafood.

Americans have borrowed from these cuisines and many of the European dishes are now part of our appetizer repertoire. In general, however, we favor easy-to-prepare finger foods, or perhaps a small portion of a flavorful dish. Appetizers are a definite part of our entertainment schedule. They may be served with beverages before a meal, or in lieu of a first course at the table.

Snappy Clam Dip

1 can (10½ ounces) condensed
  cream of celery soup
1 package (8 ounces) cream
  cheese, softened

1 can (7½ ounces) minced clams,
  well-drained
1 tablespoon chopped parsley
2 teaspoons horseradish

With rotary beater or slow speed of mixer, blend soup into cream cheese. Beat just until blended. Mix in clams, parsley, and horseradish. Chill. Serve with crackers or chips. Makes 2½ cups dip.

Eggs a la Russe

1 can (10½ ounces) condensed
  cream of celery soup
¼ cup mayonnaise
¼ cup chili sauce
1 tablespoon chopped stuffed
  olives

1 tablespoon minced onion
1 tablespoon chopped parsley
1 teaspoon dried chives
1 teaspoon lemon juice
Dash hot pepper sauce
6 hard-cooked eggs, halved

Combine all ingredients except eggs. Chill. For each serving, arrange 2 egg halves flat side down on dish; top with about ¼ cup sauce. 6 servings.

❋ Cocktail Meatballs or Frankfurters

1 pound ground beef
2 tablespoons bread crumbs
1 egg, slightly beaten
½ teaspoon salt
½ cup finely chopped onion
⅓ cup finely chopped green pepper
2 tablespoons butter or margarine

1 can (10¾ ounces) condensed
  tomato soup
2 tablespoons brown sugar
1 tablespoon vinegar
1 tablespoon Worcestershire
1 teaspoon prepared mustard
Dash hot pepper sauce

So simple and so good, these meatballs can be shaped and refrigerated hours before the party. Then it's a breeze to brown and bake them in sauce shortly before serving.

Mix beef, bread crumbs, egg, and salt; shape into 50 small meatballs (½ inch). Place in shallow baking pan (13x9x2 inches). Broil until browned; turn once. Spoon off fat. Meanwhile, in saucepan, cook onion and green pepper in butter until tender. Stir in remaining ingredients. Pour over meatballs. Cover; bake at 350° F. for 20 minutes. Makes 50 meatballs for appetizers.

Cocktail Frankfurters: Substitute 1½ pounds frankfurters, cut in 1-inch pieces for meatball mixture. Proceed as above.

Crab on Toast

¼ cup finely chopped green onion
¼ cup finely chopped green
  pepper
2 small cloves garlic, minced
2 tablespoons butter or margarine
1 can (10½ ounces) condensed
  cream of mushroom soup
1½ cups flaked cooked crab meat

2 tablespoons finely chopped ripe
  olives
1 teaspoon lemon juice
Generous dash hot pepper sauce
20 slices toast, cut in half
  diagonally*
¾ cup shredded Cheddar, Swiss,
  or grated Parmesan cheese

In saucepan, cook onion, green pepper, and garlic in butter until tender. Stir in remaining ingredients except toast and cheese. Place 1 tablespoon crab mixture on each piece of toast. Top each with cheese. Broil 4 inches from heat until cheese melts. Makes 40 appetizers.

*Or use 40 slices melba toast or whole rye crackers.

Liver Pate

Pate:

2 packages (8 ounces each)
  frozen chicken livers
1 can (10½ ounces) condensed
  cream of mushroom soup
1 cup chopped onion

2 eggs
¼ cup milk
⅛ teaspoon pepper
⅛ teaspoon thyme, crushed
¼ cup fine dry bread crumbs

In saucepan, cook frozen livers in boiling water 15 minutes or until done; drain. In blender at high speed, beat soup, onion, eggs, milk, pepper, and thyme until smooth. At low speed, gradually add livers and bread crumbs. Pour into loaf pan (8x4x3 inches); place in shallow pan with 1-inch deep water. Bake at 325°F. for 1½ hours or until silver knife inserted in center comes out clean. *Refrigerate overnight.*

Glaze:

2 tablespoons butter or margarine
2 tablespoons flour
½ cup chicken broth
2 teaspoons unflavored gelatine

¼ cup water
2 tablespoons heavy cream
Generous dash white pepper
Parsley

In saucepan, melt butter; blend in flour. Gradually add broth. Cook, stirring until thickened and smooth. In small saucepan, sprinkle gelatine over water; stir over low heat until gelatine is dissolved. Blend into sauce with cream and pepper. *Cool to room temperature.*

Unmold pate. Pour glaze evenly over top and sides. (Glaze should set on contact with *chilled* pate). Garnish with parsley. 10 to 12 servings.

Pâté, meaning in French "pie," may be served hot or cold. Achieve variety by cooking in molds of different shapes and by using pretty garnishes like vegetable strips, flowers, slices, rings or dices. Serve attractively.

❋ Cheese Fondue
Recipe may be doubled

½ cup Sauterne or other dry
    white wine
1 medium clove garlic, minced
4 slices (4 ounces)
    natural Swiss cheese, torn in
    pieces

2 tablespoons flour
1 can (10¾ ounces) condensed
    Cheddar cheese soup
French or Italian bread cubes*

In saucepan or fondue pot, simmer wine and garlic. Combine cheese and flour; gradually blend into wine. Heat until cheese melts; stir now and then. Blend in soup; heat, stirring until smooth. Spear bread with fork or toothpick and dip into fondue. Makes 2 cups.

*Also good with bite-size pieces of cooked franks, lobster, shrimp, or artichoke hearts.

Appetizer Veal Roll-Ups

1½ pounds veal cutlet, thinly
    sliced
24 canned whole small mushroom
    caps (about 4½ ounces)
¼ cup chopped onion
1 tablespoon chopped parsley

2 tablespoons butter or margarine
1 can (10½ ounces) condensed
    cream of chicken soup
¼ cup water
2 tablespoons Madeira wine

Pound veal with meat hammer or edge of heavy saucer. Cut into 24 pieces (about 2½ inches square). Wrap 1 mushroom cap in each piece veal; fasten with toothpicks or skewers. In skillet, brown roll-ups and cook onion with parsley in butter until tender. Stir in remaining ingredients. Cover; cook over low heat 30 minutes or until veal is tender. Makes 24 small roll-ups.

Blue Cheese Dip

1 package (8 ounces) cream
    cheese, softened
1 can (10½ ounces) condensed
    cream of celery soup

½ cup crumbled blue cheese
¼ cup diced cucumber

Beat cream cheese until smooth; blend in soup. Stir in blue cheese and cucumber. Chill. Serve with crackers or chips. Makes 2½ cups dip.

Serve dips in pretty bowls or in a handsome curly-leafed Savoy cabbage (hollowed out). Vary the dunkers, using creative crackers, toast triangles, vegetable sticks or as in the Middle East, "scoops" of lettuce or cabbage.

Invite guests to a sip and dip party starring this Cheese Fondue in a pretty earthenware pot or heavy chafing dish. Offer it with a light dry white wine before a crackling fire.

SOUPS

Close to the hearts of all of us is the marvelous repertoire of savory soups, which can be enjoyed hot or cold on any occasion, and at anytime of day. Broth, consomme, puree, bisque, potage, bouillon or chowder, clear, creamed or thick, soup is a never-fail gastronomic winner. Reliable as an old and trusted friend, it also has the appeal and sparkle of a new acquaintance.

The saga of soup is as old as man himself. For it was pre-historic man who began the art of making soup by dropping some bones, meat, water and heated stones into an animal-skin bag. By the Stone Age soups were simmered in kettles or pots over fires. Thus *Pot au Feu* (Pot on the Fire) was created. The first soup mentioned in writing was made with lentils, the "mess of pottage" for which Esau sold his birthright to Jacob.

For a very long time soup was called potage, broth, brewis or gruel. Its present name was taken from "soppers," which were the bread pieces dipped into meat broth. To soups we are indebted for the name of "restaurant." For in 1765 a Parisian tavern proprietor, one Boulanger, started selling nourishing soups, which he called *restorantes*, restorative snacks or pick-ups.

Over the years the world-wide appeal of soups has transcended geographic and social boundaries. Every country has one or more national favorites. Soup may be basic and robust or complex and subtle. In the old days the stockpot always simmered on the back of the stove, and America is justly proud of the regional specialties its cooks created, as well as many favorites from foreign lands.

Today, you—as cook and hostess—have a dazzling variety of prepared soups immediately available. Delectable in themselves, you can quickly and imaginatively make your own new soup creations by combining two or more of them. There are many popular soup-mates and the combinations are endless. Such is the versatility of soup that a nuance of flavor or a bit of color may give an old favorite fresh appeal and attraction. You may work wonders with a touch of spice, a dash of Sherry, a sprinkling of herbs, grated cheese, toasted nuts or croutons, or a dollop of sour or whipped cream.

Let it be steaming hot or frosty cold. Serving soup is fun. Spoon it from a large bowl, pour it from a pitcher, or ladle it from a tureen.

Soup is a standby for all social occasions. As a prelude to a meal, a delicate first course or a main dish. Its warming goodness is delicious with salads or sandwiches. As a snack it is perfect from midmorning to midnight. Soup is the answer to coping with unexpected guests, and is excellent for entertaining large numbers.

TAKE YOUR CHOICE

Are the children hungry but uninterested? Chicken & stars, tomato-beef noodle-O's, chicken noodle-O's and chicken 'n dumplings will intrigue and nourish. So will "Souper-snacks" made with cream of chicken, green pea or vegetable.

Is the male animal roaring for his food? Call on the "Manhandlers," such as bean with bacon, beef, chili beef, minestrone, noodles & ground beef, split pea with ham, clam chowder (Manhattan-style or New England), oyster stew, Scotch broth or vegetable beef.

Does the menu for a special dinner party need a first course? Sophisticated golden mushroom, black bean, cream of mushroom or consomme will set the pace with distinction.

Are the bathroom scales out of order? Possibly. But try the "Slim Six" before buying new scales. Beef broth, chicken broth, chicken gumbo, consomme, onion and old fashioned vegetable...each is under 60 calories per seven-ounce cup.

Is the household budget out of balance? Soup can't solve the problem but it has always helped.

To broaden your acquaintance with appealing soups, here are serving ideas and specialties from our collection.

Souper Snacks

Need a wee morsel to sustain you through the next 2 hours before dinner or to welcome the children home from school? And what do you serve when the bridge players stay late but vote down the standard rich dessert with coffee routine? Reach to the soup shelf for a snack that's warming and always pleasingly good.

Is your preference for "Soup and Crackers"... or are you in favor of "Soup and Crunch," such as piping hot tomato alongside golden carrot sticks? With mixing and matching, you're bound to come up with just the right tidbit to suit snackers.

Chicken 'n Dumplings............*Apple slices sandwiched with peanut butter*
Green Pea...............................*Round butter crackers or saltines*
Chicken Noodle ....*Popcorn or peanuts*
Vegetable ....*Bologna rolled around pickle strip*
Chili Beef...............................*Green pepper rings or corn chips*
Onion ....*Celery filled with cottage cheese or shredded wheat crackers*
Cream of Potato..*Fresh orange wedges*
Golden Vegetable Noodle-O's.................................*Cheese cubes*

Chinese Noodle Soup

1 cup sliced mushrooms
   (about ¼ pound)
2 tablespoons butter or margarine
2 cans (10½ ounces each)
   condensed beef noodle soup

2 soup cans water
1½ cups cooked shrimp
2 tablespoons chopped watercress
4 teaspoons soy sauce

In saucepan, brown mushrooms in butter. Add remaining ingredients. Heat; stir now and then. 4 to 6 servings.

Pennsylvania Dutch Chowder

½ cup sliced celery
½ cup chopped onion
2 tablespoons butter or margarine
2 cans (10½ ounces each) condensed chicken 'n dumplings
   soup

1½ soup cans water
1 can (8 ounces) whole kernel
   corn
Generous dash pepper

In saucepan, cook celery and onion in butter until tender. Add remaining ingredients. Heat; stir now and then. 4 to 6 servings.

This hearty dish probably originated in New England but today each American locale has a specialty. The name derives from France where a chaudière is a short-legged kettle.

Pasta Fagioli

2 tablespoons chopped parsley
1/4 teaspoon rosemary, crushed
1 medium clove garlic, minced
2 tablespoons olive oil
1 can (11½ ounces) condensed
  bean with bacon soup

1 soup can water
1 teaspoon tomato paste
Generous dash pepper
½ cup cooked elbow macaroni

In saucepan, cook parsley, rosemary, and garlic in oil until parsley is wilted. Stir in soup, water, tomato paste, and pepper; add macaroni. Heat; stir now and then. 2 to 3 servings.

Potage Senegalese

1 can (10½ ounces) condensed
  cream of chicken soup
1 soup can water
½ cup light cream
¼ cup applesauce

2 tablespoons shredded coconut
1 teaspoon curry powder
½ teaspoon garlic salt
½ teaspoon onion powder
1 avocado, sliced

In saucepan, combine all ingredients except avocado. Heat; stir now and then. Top each serving with avocado. 3 servings.

For chilled soup: Prepare recipe as above; chill 4 to 6 hours. Serve in chilled bowls.

Black Bean Double Hot

1/3 cup chopped onion
2 tablespoons butter or margarine
1 can (10½ ounces) condensed
  black bean soup
1 soup can water

2 teaspoons chopped hot cherry
  peppers
1 teaspoon lemon or lime juice
¼ cup coarsely crushed tortilla
  chips
Lime slices

In saucepan, cook onion in butter until tender. Stir in soup; gradually blend in water. Add peppers and lemon or lime juice. Heat; stir now and then. Just before serving, stir in tortilla chips. Garnish with lime slices. 2 to 3 servings.

Consomme Parfait

1 can (10½ ounces) condensed
  consomme

¼ cup yogurt
2 tablespoons chopped parsley

Place unopened can of consomme in refrigerator until jellied, at least 4 hours. To serve, spoon consomme in small sherbet glasses; top with yogurt and chopped parsley. 2 to 3 servings.

Vegetable Salami Chowder

½ cup salami strips
2 tablespoons butter or margarine
1 can (10¾ ounces) condensed
   old fashioned vegetable soup

1 soup can water
½ cup chopped canned tomatoes
1 teaspoon prepared horseradish
Garlic flavored croutons

In saucepan, brown salami in butter. Add soup, water, tomatoes, and horseradish. Heat; stir now and then. Garnish with croutons. 2 to 3 servings.

French Onion Soup

1 can (10½ ounces) condensed
   onion soup
1 soup can water

3 thin slices French bread, toasted
¾ cup grated Gruyere or Swiss
   cheese

In saucepan, combine soup and water; heat. In individual serving bowls, place a slice of French bread; top with cheese. Pour in hot soup. 2 to 3 servings.

Broiler Method: Pour heated soup into individual oven-proof serving bowls. Place bread on top; sprinkle with cheese. Broil until cheese melts.

This soup's main ingredient was once a "weather predictor" according to an old rhyme. "Onion's skin is very thin, Mild weather's coming in, Onion's skin is thick and tough, Coming winter's cold and rough."

Marriage Soup Italiano

1 can (10½ ounces) condensed
   cream of chicken soup
1 cup light cream

1 can (10½ ounces) condensed
   chicken noodle soup
½ cup milk
2 tablespoons grated Parmesan cheese

In saucepan, blend cream of chicken soup and cream; add remaining ingredients. Heat; stir now and then. 2 to 3 servings.

Tropical Fruit Soup

1 can (10½ ounces) condensed
   cream of chicken soup, chilled
½ cup mashed ripe banana
1 soup can milk
1 teaspoon lime juice

Grated lime rind or toasted
   slivered almonds or coconut
Nutmeg
½ cup halved seeded white grapes

Stir soup; gradually blend in banana, milk, and lime juice. Garnish with rind, almonds, or coconut, and nutmeg. Serve with grapes. 3 to 4 servings.

Pages 20-21: America's favorite lunch...Soup and Sandwiches.
Soups shown are: Split Pea Potage, Chicken-Vegetable Noodle-O's,
Barbecue Bean and California Bisque.

❋ Split Pea Potage

¼ cup chopped onion
1 medium clove garlic, minced
2 tablespoons butter or margarine
1 can (11¼ ounces) condensed
   split pea with ham soup

1 soup can water
2 tablespoons Sherry
½ cup chopped canned tomatoes

In saucepan, cook onion with garlic in butter until tender. Stir in soup; gradually blend in water. Add Sherry and tomatoes. Heat; stir now and then. 2 to 3 servings.

❋ Vichyssoise

1 can (10½ ounces) condensed
   cream of potato soup

1 soup can milk or ½ light cream
   and ½ milk
Chopped chives, mint, or parsley

In saucepan, combine soup and milk. Heat; stir now and then. Beat until smooth with blender; or use rotary beater or electric mixer and strain. Chill 4 hours or more. Thin to desired consistency. Serve in chilled bowls. Garnish with chives, mint, or parsley. 2 to 3 servings.

"Soup puts the heart at ease, calms down the violence of hunger, eliminates the tensions of the day, and awakens and refines the appetite."
ESCOFFIER.

❋ Barbecue Bean Soup

½ cup green pepper strips
⅓ cup chopped onion
1 medium clove garlic, minced
2 tablespoons butter or margarine
1 can (11 ounces) condensed hot
   dog bean soup

1 soup can water
1 tablespoon chili sauce or
   ketchup
½ teaspoon prepared mustard
⅛ teaspoon hot pepper sauce

In saucepan, cook pepper and onion with garlic in butter until tender. Stir in soup; gradually blend in water. Add remaining ingredients. Heat; stir now and then. 2 to 3 servings.

California Bisque

¼ cup thinly sliced celery
1 tablespoon butter or margarine
1 can (11 ounces) condensed
   bisque of tomato soup

1 soup can water
½ medium avocado, diced
2 teaspoons lemon juice

In saucepan, cook celery in butter until tender. Add remaining ingredients. Heat; stir now and then. 2 to 3 servings.

Oyster Stew Orientale

½ cup chopped onion
2 tablespoons butter or margarine
1 can (10¼ ounces) condensed
    oyster stew
1 soup can milk

1 tablespoon toasted sesame
    seeds
¾ cup cooked rice
Chopped chives

In saucepan, cook onion in butter until tender. Add soup, milk, and sesame seeds. Heat; stir now and then. Serve about ¼ cup rice in each bowl. Garnish with chives. 2 to 3 servings.

Caldo Verde

2 cups spinach leaves cut in thin
    strips
1 tablespoon olive oil

1 can (10½ ounces) condensed
    cream of potato soup
1 soup can water
Generous dash hot pepper sauce

In saucepan, cook spinach in olive oil until tender. Stir in soup, water, and pepper sauce. Heat; stir now and then. 3 servings.

Pot-o-Gold Soup

1 can (10½ ounces) condensed
    chicken broth
3 cups sliced raw carrots (about
    1 pound)
¼ cup chopped celery

2 tablespoons chopped onion
1 soup can light cream
½ soup can milk
¼ teaspoon nutmeg

In saucepan, combine broth, carrots, celery, and onion. Cover; cook 20 minutes or until carrots are very tender. Blend in electric blender until smooth. In saucepan, combine all ingredients. Heat; stir now and then. 3 to 4 servings.

For chilled soup: Chill 3 to 4 hours or overnight. Thin to desired consistency with additional cold milk.

Spanish Garlic Soup

2 medium cloves garlic
2 tablespoons olive oil
2 thin slices French bread

1 can (10½ ounces) condensed
    beef broth
1 soup can water
1 egg, slightly beaten

In saucepan, slowly brown garlic in oil; remove garlic. Add bread; brown. Add broth and water. Cook over low heat 5 minutes; stir to break up bread. Bring to boil; pour egg slowly into soup, stirring constantly. 2 to 3 servings.

Won Ton Soup

1 egg, slightly beaten
½ teaspoon water
⅓ cup flour
¼ teaspoon salt
½ cup finely chopped chicken
1 tablespoon finely chopped
   green onion

1 teaspoon soy sauce
2 cans (10½ ounces each)
   condensed chicken broth
2 soup cans water
½ cup cooked chicken or pork
   cut in strips
¼ cup chopped spinach

Gradually stir 2 tablespoons egg and ½ teaspoon water into flour and salt. Knead on lightly floured board until dough is smooth; roll dough to 10x7½-inch piece; cut into 12 squares (2½ inch). Thoroughly mix finely chopped chicken, onion, soy, and remaining egg; place a heaping teaspoon of mixture on each square. Bring corners together and seal edges. In saucepan, combine soup and water; bring to boil. Add won tons; cook over low heat 5 minutes. Add chicken or pork and spinach. 4 servings.

Greek Soup

1 can (10½ ounces) condensed
   chicken with rice soup
1 soup can water

1 egg
1 tablespoon lemon juice
Lemon slices

In saucepan or double boiler, combine soup and water. Cook over *medium heat*. Remove from heat. In a bowl, beat egg until light and frothy; gradually add lemon juice and 1 cup hot broth. Slowly stir egg mixture into soup. Cook a few minutes over *very low heat*, stirring until egg is thoroughly blended with soup. *Do not boil*. Garnish with lemon. Serve immediately. (Overheating will cause curdling.) 2 to 3 servings.

Stracciatella

1 can (10½ ounces) condensed
   chicken broth
1 soup can water
1 egg

2 tablespoons grated Parmesan
   cheese
1 tablespoon chopped parsley
Dash nutmeg, optional

In saucepan, combine broth and water. Heat. Beat egg with cheese, parsley, and nutmeg; gradually pour into simmering soup, stirring gently until egg is set. Serve immediately. 2 to 3 servings.

Richly red Tomato Soup warms all occasions. Little folks and oldsters welcome its cheering appearance and irresistible flavor. Serve with finesse and flair from a handsome tureen.

❋ *Zuppa Zingara*

½ pound beef tenderloin or
    sirloin, cut in very thin strips
2 tablespoons salad oil
1 can (10½ ounces) condensed
    golden mushroom soup
2 cans (10½ ounces each)
    condensed onion soup

1½ soup cans water
¼ cup Burgundy or other dry
    red wine
2 tablespoons chopped parsley
⅛ teaspoon tarragon, crushed

In saucepan, brown beef in oil. Pour off fat. Stir in golden mushroom soup; gradually blend in remaining ingredients. Heat; stir now and then. 6 to 8 servings.

Vegetable Beef 'n Herb Soup

1 tablespoon finely chopped
    parsley
¼ teaspoon basil, crushed
1 small clove garlic, minced

1 tablespoon butter or margarine
1 can (10¾ ounces) condensed
    vegetable beef soup
1 soup can water
Grated Parmesan cheese

In saucepan, cook parsley and basil with garlic in butter until tender. Add soup and water. Heat; stir now and then. Serve with Parmesan. 2 to 3 servings.

Offer soup in flowered cups, colorful mugs, or sturdy glasses, deep plates or bowls. For a large party a chafing dish may double as a server-warmer for soup.

Soup Mates

Mix two soups to make a new soup. Most everyone enjoys concocting their own variation by mixing and matching different kinds.

Celery Pea Potage

1 can (10½ ounces) condensed
    cream of celery soup
1 can (11¼ ounces) condensed
    green pea soup

1 soup can milk
1 soup can water

In saucepan, stir soups until smooth; gradually blend in milk and water. Heat; stir now and then. 4 to 6 servings.

Beef and Vegetable Noodle-O's

1 can (11 ounces) condensed
    tomato-beef noodle-O's soup

1 can (10¾ ounces) condensed
    vegetable soup
2 soup cans water

In saucepan, combine all ingredients. Heat; stir now and then. 4 to 6 servings.

All-Star Chicken Soup

1 can (10½ ounces) condensed
chicken 'n dumplings soup

1 can (10½ ounces) condensed
chicken & stars soup
1½ soup cans water

In saucepan, combine all ingredients. Heat; stir now and then. 4 servings.

Beef-Eater's Bowl

1 can (10½ ounces) condensed
golden mushroom soup

1 can (10¾ ounces) condensed
noodles & ground beef soup
1½ soup cans water

In saucepan, combine all ingredients. Heat; stir now and then. 4 servings.

Double Chicken Soup

1 can (10½ ounces) condensed
cream of chicken soup
1 can (10¾ ounces) condensed
chicken vegetable soup

1 soup can milk
½ soup can water

In saucepan, combine all ingredients. Heat; stir now and then. 4 servings.

Stouthearted Stockpot

1 can (10½ ounces) condensed
golden mushroom soup

1 can (10¾ ounces) condensed
vegetable and beef stockpot soup
2 soup cans water

In saucepan, combine all ingredients. Heat; stir now and then. 4 to 6 servings.

Chicken-Vegetable Noodle-O's

1 can (10¾ ounces) condensed
chicken vegetable soup

1 can (10½ ounces) condensed
golden vegetable noodle-O's soup
2 soup cans water

In saucepan, combine all ingredients. Heat; stir now and then. 4 to 6 servings.

Creamy Chicken Noodle-O's

1 can (10½ ounces) condensed
cream of chicken soup
1 can (10½ ounces) condensed
chicken noodle-O's soup

1 soup can milk
½ soup can water

In saucepan, combine all ingredients. Heat; stir now and then. 4 servings.

BEEF

"**W**hen in doubt, serve beef" might well be the motto of the modern hostess. Certainly there is no question that beef is the most popular meat in America. Fortunately, it is available in fascinating variety, and you may prepare any number of inviting dishes from a cosmopolitan collection of recipes. Whether braised, roasted, stewed, broiled, baked or barbecued, beef is sure to be a triumph for any social occasion.

Paradoxically, our favorite meat is not native to this hemisphere, since the first cattle came from Europe. Those brought by the Spaniards to the Southwest developed into the world-famous Texas Longhorns and provided not only necessary fare, but colorful folklore as well. The romance of the Western cowboys and their chuck-wagon cookery is a bright page of history and legend.

The various cuts of beef, numbering as many as 45, differ, of course, in quality and flavor. Such superb fare as a standing rib roast or a filet mignon, however, is no more nutritious than a boneless pot roast or a chuck steak.

Two particular beef specialties, steaks and hamburgers, have become national symbols, and their current international popularity is generally associated with America. Steak, however, was a favorite in Merrie Englande, deriving its name from a Saxon term, *on steik*, "a slice of meat roasted on a spit." Ground meats have also been enjoyed through the ages, and our hamburgers were named for the bustling German seaport of Hamburg.

Fortunately, beef has a cosmopolitan appeal, and our gastronomic beef repertoire includes superb dishes from many lands. Modern menu makers have many ways to flavor beef with herbs, spices, wines and sauces. And, these days, convenience foods play a major role in shortening the time it takes to prepare these appealing extra touches.

❋ Beef Burgundy

1 pound sirloin cut into 1-inch
    cubes
2 tablespoons butter or margarine
1 can (10½ ounces) condensed
    golden mushroom soup
¼ cup Burgundy or other dry
    red wine

12 small whole white onions
    (¾ pound)
2 tablespoons chopped parsley
⅛ teaspoon pepper
Cooked wide noodles

In skillet, brown meat in butter. Add remaining ingredients except noodles. Cover; cook over low heat 1 hour or until tender. Stir now and then. Serve with noodles. 4 servings.

❋ Hungarian Goulash

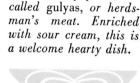

In Hungary a variety of flavorful dishes, each seasoned with paprika, are called gulyas, or herdsman's meat. Enriched with sour cream, this is a welcome hearty dish.

1½ pounds beef cubes (1½ inch)
2 tablespoons shortening
1 can (10¾ ounces) condensed
    tomato soup
½ cup sour cream
¾ cup water

1 cup sliced onion
1 tablespoon paprika
⅛ teaspoon pepper
4 medium potatoes (1 pound),
    quartered

In large heavy pan, brown beef in shortening; pour off fat. Stir in remaining ingredients except potatoes. Cover; cook over low heat 1½ hours. Stir now and then. Add potatoes. Cover; cook over low heat 1 hour more or until meat is tender. Stir now and then. 4 servings.

Savory Meatball 'n Spaghetti Bake

1½ pounds ground beef
½ cup fine dry bread crumbs
1 egg, slightly beaten
1 teaspoon salt
1 cup sliced onion
2 tablespoons shortening
2 cans (10½ ounces each)
    condensed cream of
    mushroom soup

1 cup sour cream
1 cup chopped tomatoes
1 medium cucumber, cut in
    cubes (about 2 cups)
1½ cups spaghetti broken in 2-inch
    pieces, cooked and drained
½ teaspoon dried dill leaves,
    crushed
Grated Parmesan cheese

In large bowl, combine beef, crumbs, egg, and salt; shape into 24 meatballs. In a large skillet or 2 skillets (about 10 inch), brown meatballs and cook onion in shortening until tender; pour off fat. Blend in soup, sour cream, and tomatoes. Add cucumber, spaghetti, and dill; mix well. Bake in two 1½-quart casseroles at 350°F. for 30 minutes or until hot. Sprinkle with cheese. 6 servings.

Salisbury Steak, Onion Gravy

1 can (10½ ounces) condensed
    onion soup
1½ pounds ground beef
½ cup fine dry bread crumbs
1 egg, slightly beaten
¼ teaspoon salt

Dash pepper
1 tablespoon flour
¼ cup ketchup
¼ cup water
1 teaspoon Worcestershire
½ teaspoon prepared mustard

In bowl, combine ⅓ cup soup with beef, crumbs, egg, salt, pepper. Shape into 6 oval patties. In skillet, brown patties; pour off fat. Gradually blend remaining soup into flour until smooth. Add to skillet with remaining ingredients; stir to loosen browned bits. Cover; cook over low heat 20 minutes or until done. Stir now and then. 6 servings.

Barbecue Stew

1½ pounds beef cubes (1½ inch)
2 tablespoons shortening
1 can (10½ ounces) condensed
    beef broth
½ cup water
1 cup sliced onion
¼ cup ketchup
1 tablespoon prepared mustard
1 large clove garlic, minced

Dash hot pepper sauce
½ teaspoon salt
Generous dash pepper
1 small green pepper, cut into
    1-inch squares
1½ cups thickly sliced
    mushrooms (about ¼ pound)
Tomato wedges

In skillet, brown meat in shortening; pour off fat. Add broth, water, onion, ketchup, mustard, garlic, hot pepper sauce, and seasonings. Cover; cook over low heat 2 hours. Add green pepper and mushrooms; cook 30 minutes more or until meat is tender. Stir now and then. Thicken if desired. Garnish with tomato. 4 servings.

❋ Roast Beef El Capitan
Pictured on front cover

4-pound rolled rib roast
½ cup cooked ham strips
2 medium cloves garlic, minced

1 can (10½ ounces) condensed
    golden mushroom soup
¾ cup water
1 teaspoon capers (optional)

Place meat, fat-side up, in large roasting pan. Roast at 325°F. for 1 hour 40 minutes or until desired doneness (medium—about 25 minutes per pound or 160°F. on meat thermometer). Remove meat from pan; pour off excess fat, saving drippings. On top of range, in roasting pan, brown ham with garlic in drippings. Add soup; stir to loosen browned bits. Add water and capers. Heat; stir now and then. After slicing meat, add meat juices to gravy. 6 to 8 servings.

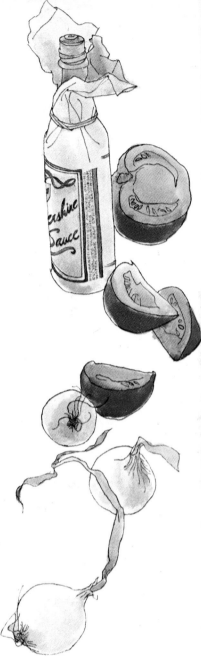

31

❋ Best Ever Meat Loaf

1 can (10½ ounces) condensed
   cream of mushroom or golden
   mushroom soup
2 pounds ground beef
½ cup fine dry bread crumbs

⅓ cup finely chopped onion
1 egg, slightly beaten
1 teaspoon salt
⅓ cup water
2 to 3 tablespoons drippings

Mix thoroughly ½ cup soup, beef, bread crumbs, onion, egg, and salt. Shape firmly into loaf (8x4 inches); place in shallow baking pan. Bake at 375°F. for 1 hour 15 minutes. Blend remaining soup, water, and drippings. Heat; stir now and then. Serve with loaf. 6 servings.

Frosted Meat Loaf: Prepare loaf as above; bake for 1 hour. Frost loaf with 4 cups mashed potatoes; sprinkle with shredded Cheddar cheese. Bake 15 minutes more.

Swedish Meat Loaf: Add ½ teaspoon nutmeg to loaf. Blend remaining soup with ⅓ cup sour cream; omit drippings and water. Serve over loaf; sprinkle with additional nutmeg. Garnish with thinly sliced cucumber.

Meat Loaf Wellington:
Crescent Rolls (*Refrigerated*): Prepare loaf as above. Bake at 375°F. for 1 hour. Spoon off fat. Separate 1 package (8 ounces) refrigerated crescent dinner rolls; place crosswise over top and down sides of meat loaf, overlapping slightly. Bake 15 minutes more.

Patty Shells: Thaw 1 package (10 ounces) frozen puff pastry patty shells. Prepare loaf as above. Bake at 375°F. for 30 minutes. Spoon off fat. Increase oven temperature to 400°F. On floured board, roll 5 patty shells into rectangle (12x8 inches); prick several times with fork. Cover top and sides of loaf with pastry. Decorate top with remaining patty shell, rolled and cut into fancy shapes. Bake for 45 minutes more or until golden brown. Serve with sauce.

Perfect Pot-Luck Casserole

1 pound ground beef
⅓ cup chopped onion
1 cup shredded Cheddar cheese
1 can (10¾ ounces) condensed
   tomato soup

2 cups cooked medium noodles
1 cup cooked corn
¼ cup water
1 teaspoon mustard
1 teaspoon salt

In saucepan, brown beef and cook onion until tender; stir to separate meat. Pour off fat. Stir in ¾ cup cheese and remaining ingredients. Spoon into 1½-quart casserole; top with remaining cheese. Bake at 350°F. for 30 minutes. 4 servings.

Green Bean: Substitute 1 cup cooked cut green beans for corn.

A simplified version of the classic Beef Wellington is
Meatloaf Wellington *made quickly with refrigerated crescent rolls.*
Doubly good with Golden Mushroom Sauce.

❋ Super Rolled Meat Loaf

2 cans (10½ ounces each)
   condensed cream of mushroom
   soup
3 pounds ground beef
½ cup finely chopped onion
2 cups small bread cubes
2 eggs, slightly beaten
8 slices (8 ounces) boiled ham

8 slices (8 ounces) Swiss cheese
½ medium green pepper, cut in
   strips
Generous dash tarragon
1 tablespoon butter or margarine
⅓ cup water
½ cup chopped canned tomatoes

Combine 1 cup soup, beef, onion, bread cubes, and eggs. *Mix thoroughly*. Divide in half. On waxed paper, pat into two 12x9-inch pieces. Press ham and cheese into each to within 1 inch of edges. With aid of waxed paper, roll meat tightly jelly-roll fashion starting at long edges. Seal ends; use waxed paper to transfer to shallow baking dishes. Bake at 350°F. for 1 hour. Meanwhile, in saucepan, cook green pepper with tarragon in butter until tender. Add remaining soup, water, and tomatoes. Heat; stir now and then. Serve with loaves. 12 servings.

❋ Many Way Meatballs

1 pound ground beef
¼ cup fine dry bread crumbs
¼ cup finely chopped onion
1 egg, slightly beaten
¼ teaspoon salt

1 can (10¾ ounces) condensed
   Cheddar cheese, cream of celery
   or mushroom, golden mushroom,
   tomato or vegetable soup
½ cup water
2 tablespoons chopped parsley

Mix beef, bread crumbs, onion, egg, and salt; shape into 16 meatballs. In skillet, brown meatballs; pour off fat. Stir in soup, water, and parsley. Cover; cook over low heat 20 minutes; stir now and then. 4 servings.

Ring Meat Loaf with Tomato-Cheese Topping

6 slices bacon
½ cup finely chopped onion
1 can (10¾ ounces) condensed
   tomato soup
1½ pounds ground beef
½ cup fine dry bread crumbs
   or 1 cup cooked rice

¼ cup chopped parsley
1 egg, slightly beaten
⅛ teaspoon pepper
2 slices (2 ounces) process
   cheese, split diagonally

In skillet, cook bacon; remove and crumble. Cook onion in 2 tablespoons bacon drippings until tender. Mix thoroughly with ½ can soup, beef, crumbs, parsley, egg, bacon, and pepper. In shallow baking dish (13x9x2 inches), shape firmly into ring (2 inches high with 4-inch opening). Bake at 350°F. for 1 hour. Spoon off fat. Top ring with remaining soup and cheese; bake until cheese starts to melt. Remove ring with the aid of two spatulas. 6 servings.

Deluxe Crusty Meat Loaf

Pastry for 2-crust pie
1½ pounds ground beef
1 can (10½ ounces) condensed
   cream of celery soup
1 cup cooked rice
1 egg, slightly beaten
½ cup finely chopped onion
¼ cup finely chopped parsley
1 teaspoon salt

½ teaspoon tarragon, crushed
Generous dash pepper
1 cup sliced mushrooms (about ¼
   pound)
1 small clove garlic, minced
2 tablespoons butter or margarine
¼ cup milk
2 tablespoons Madeira

Roll pastry into a rectangle (16x11 inches). Combine beef, ¼ cup soup, rice, egg, onion, parsley, salt, tarragon, and pepper. Lengthwise on pastry, lightly shape beef mixture into loaf (11x3 inches). Cover entire loaf with pastry by overlapping and sealing long edges on top of loaf. Fold up ends and seal. Turn loaf seamside down on well-greased baking sheet or shallow baking dish; brush with milk. Make several slits on top and sides of loaf. Bake at 375°F. for 1 hour. Remove, using 2 spatulas. Meanwhile, in saucepan, cook mushrooms and garlic in butter until tender. Add remaining soup, milk, and Madeira. Heat; stir now and then. Serve with loaf. 6 servings.

✳ Skillet Meat Loaf

1 can (10¾ ounces) condensed
   tomato soup
1½ pounds ground beef
½ cup fine dry bread crumbs
1 egg, slightly beaten
¼ cup finely chopped onion
1 teaspoon salt

Generous dash pepper
1 tablespoon shortening
¼ cup water
½ teaspoon prepared mustard
2 slices (2 ounces) process
   cheese, cut in half

Combine ¼ cup soup with meat, bread crumbs, egg, onion, salt, and pepper; mix *thoroughly*. Shape *firmly* into 2 loaves. In skillet, brown loaves in shortening. Cover; cook over low heat 25 minutes. Spoon off fat. Stir in remaining soup, water, and mustard. Top loaves with cheese. Cook *uncovered* 10 minutes. Stir now and then. 6 servings.

Oven Method: Shape loaves as above. Place in a shallow baking pan. Bake at 350°F. for 40 minutes. Spoon off fat. Pour remaining soup (omit water) mixed with mustard over loaves. Top with cheese. Bake 5 minutes more.

Liver 'n Beans Piquant

4 slices bacon
1½ pounds sliced beef or calf's
    liver
2 tablespoons flour
1 can (11 ounces) condensed
    bisque of tomato soup

¾ cup water
1 package (10 ounces) frozen
    cut green beans, cooked and
    drained
⅛ teaspoon garlic salt

In skillet, cook bacon until crisp; remove. Pour off all but 2 tablespoons drippings. Dust liver with flour; brown in bacon drippings. Add soup, water, beans, and garlic salt. Cover; cook over low heat 20 minutes or until tender. Stir now and then. Garnish with bacon. 6 servings.

Old favorite foods, like friends, are ever-appealing. This adaptation of an Irish Boiled Dinner will start lots of eyes a'smiling for St. Patrick's or any other dinner.

Irish Boiled Dinner

4-pound brisket corned beef
1 can (10½ ounces) condensed
   onion soup
4 whole peppercorns
1 medium clove garlic, minced
1 bay leaf
¼ teaspoon rosemary, crushed
6 medium carrots, cut in
   1½-inch pieces

6 medium potatoes, quartered
½ cup celery cut in 1-inch
   pieces
1 medium head green cabbage,
   cut in wedges
3 tablespoons water
3 tablespoons flour

Rinse corned beef. Place in large heavy pan; add soup and seasonings. Cover; cook over low heat for 3½ hours. Add carrots, potatoes, and celery. Place cabbage on top. Cover; cook about 1 hour or until all ingredients are tender. Remove meat, vegetables, and bay leaf. Gradually blend water into flour until smooth; slowly stir into sauce. Cook, stirring until thickened. 6 to 8 servings.

Stuffed Peppers

4 medium green peppers
1 pound ground beef
½ cup chopped onion
1 can (10¾ ounces) condensed
   tomato soup
1 cup cooked rice

2 teaspoons Worcestershire
½ teaspoon salt
Generous dash pepper
2 slices (2 ounces) mild process
   or Swiss cheese, cut in strips

Remove tops and seeds from peppers; cook in boiling salted water about 5 minutes; drain. In skillet, brown beef and cook onion until tender; stir in 1 cup soup, rice, and seasonings. Spoon meat mixture into peppers; place in 1½-quart casserole. Bake at 375°F. for 25 minutes. Top with remaining soup and cheese. Bake 5 minutes more. 4 servings.

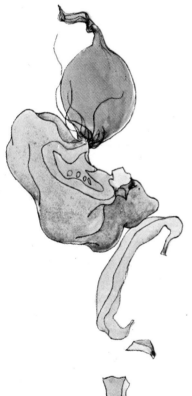

❋ Spanish Rice with Beef

1 pound ground beef
½ cup chopped onion
⅓ cup chopped green pepper
1 large clove garlic, minced
1 can (10¾ ounces) condensed
   tomato soup

1 cup water
½ cup packaged quick-cooking
   rice, uncooked*
½ teaspoon salt
2 teaspoons Worcestershire
Generous dash pepper

In skillet, brown beef and cook onion, green pepper, and garlic until vegetables are tender. Pour off fat. Add remaining ingredients. Bring to a boil. Cover; cook over low heat 15 minutes or until rice is tender. Stir now and then. 4 servings.

*If desired, substitute ⅓ cup raw regular rice for quick-cooking rice. Cook over low heat 30 minutes or until rice is tender. If necessary, add more liquid during cooking.

❋ Stuffed Cabbage Rolls

8 large cabbage leaves
1 can (10¾ ounces) condensed
   tomato soup
1 pound ground beef
1 cup cooked rice

¼ cup chopped onion
1 egg, slightly beaten
1 teaspoon salt
¼ teaspoon pepper

Cook cabbage in salted water a few minutes to soften; drain. Mix 2 tablespoons soup with remaining ingredients. Divide meat mixture among cabbage leaves; fold in sides and roll up (secure with toothpicks, if necessary). In skillet, place rolls seam side down; pour remaining soup over. Cover; cook over low heat for 40 minutes. Stir now and then, spooning sauce over rolls. 4 servings.

❋ Stuffed Flank Provencale

1½-pound flank steak
1½ cups cooked rice or 1½ cups
   cooked fine dry noodles
½ cup grated Parmesan cheese
2 tablespoons melted butter
2 tablespoons shortening
1 can (10½ ounces) condensed
   golden mushroom soup

1 can (10¾ ounces) condensed
   tomato soup
½ cup chopped onion
1 large clove garlic, minced
½ teaspoon basil, crushed
½ teaspoon oregano, crushed

An increasingly popular
lean cut flank steak comes
about ¾ inch thick and is
superb when stuffed.

Pound steak with meat hammer or edge of heavy saucer until thin. Combine rice, Parmesan, and butter. Spread mixture evenly on steak to within 1 inch of edges. Starting at narrow end, roll up; tuck in ends. Tie with string or fasten with skewers. In skillet, brown roll in shortening; pour off fat. Add remaining ingredients. Cover; cook over low heat 1 hour. Stir now and then. Turn; cook 1 hour more or until tender. Stir now and then. 6 to 8 servings.

❋ Tamale Casserole

1 pound ground beef
½ cup chopped onion
1 large clove garlic, minced
1 tablespoon chili powder
⅛ teaspoon cumin

1 can (10¾ ounces) condensed
   tomato soup
½ cup sliced ripe olives
1 can (1 pound) prepared
   tamales

In skillet, brown meat and cook onion, garlic, chili powder, and cumin until onion is tender; stir to separate meat. Add soup and olives. Pour into shallow baking dish (10x6x2 inches). Remove tamales from wrappers; arrange on top. Bake at 350°F. for 30 minutes or until hot. 4 servings.

Beef Souffle

1 can (10½ ounces) condensed
   cream of mushroom soup
½ cup shredded sharp Cheddar
   cheese
½ teaspoon marjoram, crushed

Dash cayenne
1 cup finely chopped cooked
   beef or veal
2 tablespoons chopped parsley
6 eggs, separated

In saucepan, combine soup, cheese, and seasonings. Heat slowly until cheese melts. Remove from heat; stir in beef and parsley. Beat egg yolks until thick and lemon-colored; stir into soup mixture. In large bowl, beat egg whites until soft peaks are formed; fold soup mixture into egg whites. Pour into ungreased 2-quart casserole. Bake at 300°F. for 1¼ hours or until done. Serve immediately. 4 to 6 servings.

In Japan yaki dishes are
skewered foods which are
generally broiled over
charcoal braziers. They
may be made with fish,
poultry or game, but beef
most commonly. For add-
ed pleasure, cook the
meat on a hibachi.

❋ *Teriyaki*

1 can (10½ ounces) condensed
  beef broth
¼ cup soy sauce
¼ cup diagonally sliced green
  onions

1 large clove garlic, minced
1 tablespoon brown sugar
¼ teaspoon ground ginger
1½ pounds thinly sliced sirloin
  steak (⅛-inch thick)

Combine broth, soy, green onions, garlic, brown sugar, and ginger. Cut steak into
long strips about 1-inch wide. Marinate steak for 2 hours in soup mixture. Thread
on 4 skewers. Broil about 2 inches from heat until desired doneness (5 to 10 minutes), basting with marinade and turning once. Heat remaining marinade (strain,
if desired) and serve with meat. 4 servings.

Beef Roulades Royale

1½ pounds thinly sliced round
  steak (¼-inch thick)
½ pound finely ground veal
1 egg
2 tablespoons minced onion
2 tablespoons minced parsley
⅛ teaspoon nutmeg

Generous dash pepper
6 thin carrot sticks
6 thin celery sticks
2 tablespoons shortening
1 can (10¾ ounces) condensed
  Cheddar cheese soup
½ cup chopped tomatoes

Cut steak into 6 pieces (about 6x4 inches); pound with meat hammer or edge of
heavy saucer. Thoroughly mix together veal, egg, onion, parsley, and seasonings;
divide into sixths. Place veal mixture on narrow end of meat; top with carrot and
celery stick. Roll steak; secure with toothpicks or skewers. In skillet, brown roll-
ups in shortening. Pour off fat. Add soup and tomatoes. Cover; cook over low heat
1 hour 15 minutes or until meat is tender. Stir now and then. 6 servings.

Steak Lyonnaise

1 pound round steak (½-inch
  thick)
1 tablespoon shortening
1 can (10½ ounces) condensed
  cream of celery soup

½ cup water
½ teaspoon Worcestershire
1 large clove garlic, minced
1 cup sliced onion
1 medium tomato, cut in wedges

Pound steak; cut into serving-size pieces. In skillet, brown steak in shortening;
pour off fat. Add soup, water, Worcestershire, and garlic. Cover; cook over low
heat 1 hour. Stir now and then. Add onion. Cook 30 minutes more or until tender.
Add tomato wedges; heat. 4 servings.

Saucy Steak with Parsnips

1½ pounds round steak (½-inch thick), cut in 1-inch squares
2 tablespoons shortening
1 can (10½ ounces) condensed cream of mushroom soup
1 can (10½ ounces) condensed beef broth
½ cup water
¼ cup brandy
2 tablespoons chopped pimiento
⅛ teaspoon marjoram, crushed
⅛ teaspoon thyme, crushed
1 pound parsnips, cut in 1-inch pieces (about 2 cups)

In skillet, brown round steak in shortening; pour off fat. Add remaining ingredients except parsnips. Cover; cook over low heat 1 hour. Stir. Add parsnips; cook 30 minutes more or until tender. Stir now and then. 6 servings.

London Broil with Mushroom-Tomato Sauce

1½ pound top quality flank steak
½ cup sliced onion
1 tablespoon butter or margarine
1 can (10½ ounces) condensed golden mushroom soup
⅓ cup water
⅓ cup chopped canned tomatoes
2 tablespoons chopped parsley
1 tablespoon Dijon mustard

Broil meat 2 inches from heat 5 minutes on each side. Meanwhile, in saucepan, cook onion in butter until tender. Add remaining ingredients. Heat; stir now and then. Thinly slice meat diagonally across the grain. Serve with sauce. 6 to 8 servings.

Chop Soupy

1 pound round steak, cut in very thin strips
2 tablespoons salad oil
1½ cups sliced mushrooms (¼ pound)
1½ cups diagonally sliced celery
1 cup green pepper cut in 1-inch squares
½ cup diagonally sliced green onions (1-inch pieces)*
1 can (10½ ounces) condensed beef broth or onion soup
2 tablespoons soy sauce
2 tablespoons cornstarch
½ cup water
Cooked rice

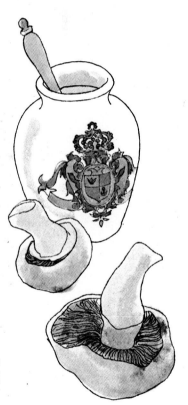

In skillet, brown beef in oil. Add vegetables, soup, and soy. Cover; cook over low heat 20 minutes or until meat is tender. Stir now and then. Blend cornstarch and water; stir into sauce. Cook, stirring until thickened. Serve with rice. 4 servings.

*Omit onions when using onion soup

❈ Meatballs Oriental

1 pound ground beef
1 cup small bread cubes
1 egg, slightly beaten
¼ cup finely chopped onion
½ teaspoon salt
¼ teaspoon allspice
1 can (12 ounces) pineapple
    chunks

½ cup diced green pepper
1 tablespoon shortening
1 can (10½ ounces) condensed
    beef broth
2 tablespoons cornstarch
⅓ cup sliced water chestnuts
¼ teaspoon ginger
Cooked rice

Great cooks create some of their greatest successes by developing a palate for seasonings....Experiment with herbs, spices, condiments, fruit juices, vinegars and flavoring extracts for your own specialties.

Mix beef, bread cubes, egg, onion, salt, and ⅛ teaspoon allspice; divide into 16 parts. Drain pineapple, saving juice. Shape meat firmly around each pineapple chunk to form meatballs. In skillet, brown meatballs and cook green pepper in shortening until tender; pour off fat. Stir in broth, ½ cup pineapple juice, cornstarch, water chestnuts, ginger, and remaining allspice. Bring to boil, stirring constantly. Cover; cook over low heat 20 minutes. Stir now and then. Serve with rice. 4 servings.

❈ Chinese Pepper Steak

1 pound round steak, cut into
    very thin strips
2 tablespoons shortening
Pepper
1 can (10½ ounces) condensed
    onion soup

½ soup can water
½ cup chopped canned tomatoes
2 teaspoons soy sauce
1 large green pepper, cut into strips
1 tablespoon cornstarch
Cooked rice

In skillet, brown steak in shortening; pour off fat. Sprinkle with pepper. Add soup, water, tomatoes, soy, and green pepper. Cover; cook over low heat 30 minutes or until tender. Stir now and then. Mix cornstarch and 2 tablespoons water until smooth; gradually stir into sauce. Cook; stir until thickened. Serve over rice. 4 servings.

❈ Easy Pot Roast

3 to 4-pound beef pot roast
1 can (10½ ounces) condensed

onion, golden mushroom, or
cream of mushroom soup

In large heavy pan, brown meat on all sides (use shortening if necessary). Pour off fat. Stir in soup. Cover; cook over low heat 2½ to 3 hours. Remove meat. To thicken, gradually blend ¼ cup water into 2 to 4 tablespoons flour. Slowly stir into soup. Cook, stirring until thickened. 6 to 8 servings.

Superb for buffet parties are Meatballs Oriental *and* Chinese Pepper Steak, *both served with rice. Each sauce is spicy and slightly sweet.*

Swiss Steak

¼ cup flour
½ teaspoon salt
Generous dash pepper
1½ pounds round steak
   (about ¾-inch thick)

2 tablespoons shortening
1 can (10¾ ounces)
   condensed vegetable soup
½ soup can water
1 cup sliced onions

Combine flour and seasonings; pound into steak with meat hammer or edge of heavy saucer. In large skillet, brown steak in shortening; pour off fat. Add remaining ingredients. Cover; cook over low heat 1 hour 15 minutes or until tender. Stir now and then. 4 servings.

❋ Stroganoff

1 pound round steak, cut into
   thin strips
½ cup sliced onion
2 tablespoons butter or margarine
1 can (10½ ounces) condensed
   golden mushroom or cream
   of mushroom soup

½ cup sour cream
½ teaspoon paprika
⅓ cup water
Hot buttered noodles

In skillet, brown meat and cook onion in butter until tender. Stir in soup, sour cream, paprika, and water. Cover; cook over low heat 45 minutes or until tender. Stir now and then. Serve over noodles. 4 servings.

❋ Beef Bourguignonne

4 slices bacon
2 pounds sirloin beef cubes
   (about 1½ inches)
2 cans (10½ ounces each)
   condensed beef broth
1 cup Burgundy or other dry
   red wine
1 large clove garlic, minced
½ teaspoon thyme, crushed

4 medium carrots, cut in half
½ pound (about 8) small whole
   white onions
2 cups sliced fresh mushrooms
   (about ½ pound)
⅓ cup water
¼ cup flour
Cooked noodles or rice
Chopped parsley

In large, heavy, oven-proof pan, cook bacon until crisp; remove and crumble. Brown beef in drippings; pour off fat. Add crumbled bacon, soup, wine, garlic, and thyme. Cover; bake at 350°F. for 1 hour 15 minutes. Add carrots, onions, and mushrooms. Bake 45 minutes more or until meat and vegetables are tender. Gradually blend water into flour until smooth; slowly stir into sauce. Cook, stirring until thickened. Serve over noodles or rice; garnish with parsley. 6 servings.

❋ Beef Roll-Ups

1½ pounds thinly sliced round
   steak (¼-inch thick)
1½ cups herb-seasoned stuffing,
   prepared as directed on package
2 tablespoons shortening

1 can (10½ ounces) condensed
   golden mushroom or cream of
   mushroom soup
½ cup water
Parsley

Cut steak into 6 pieces (about 6x4 inches); pound with meat hammer or edge of heavy saucer. Place ¼ cup stuffing near center of each piece of meat. Roll up; tuck in ends; fasten with toothpicks or skewers. In skillet, brown roll-ups in shortening; pour off fat. Stir in soup and water. Cover; cook over low heat 1¼ hours or until tender. Stir now and then. Garnish with parsley. 6 servings.

❋ Spread-a-Burger

1 can (10¾ ounces) condensed
   tomato soup
1½ pounds ground beef
⅓ cup finely chopped onion
1 tablespoon prepared mustard
1 tablespoon Worcestershire
1 teaspoon salt

1 teaspoon prepared horseradish
Dash pepper
8 frankfurter buns, split and
   toasted
8 slices (8 ounces) process
   American cheese

Combine ⅓ cup soup with remaining ingredients except buns and cheese. Spread mixture evenly over bun halves; *cover edges completely.* Broil 3 to 4 inches from heat for 5 minutes or until done. Top with remaining soup and cheese. Broil until cheese melts. Makes 8 sandwiches.

Glazed Cold Platter

1 envelope unflavored gelatine
½ cup cold water
1 can (10½ ounces) condensed
   consomme
¼ cup Madeira
2 teaspoons grated onion

5 slices cooked tongue
10 slices cooked beef
1 can (1 pound) whole baby
   carrots, drained
1 hard-cooked egg, sliced
2 stuffed olives, sliced

A decorated cold platter deserves the place of honor at your buffet table. This is a much-simplified twentieth-century version of the fanciful aspics made famous by Careme and other French chefs.

In saucepan, sprinkle gelatine on cold water to soften. Place over low heat, stirring until gelatine is dissolved. Remove from heat; stir in soup, wine, and onion. Chill until slightly thickened. Meanwhile, on a large serving platter (13x9 inches), arrange overlapping slices of tongue and beef. Garnish with carrots and egg topped with olives. Spoon a thin layer of gelatine mixture over the entire platter. Chill until set. 5 servings.

Chuck with Herb-Anchovy Sauce

3-pound boned chuck roast
   (about 2-inches thick)
1 can (10½ ounces) condensed
   cream of celery soup
½ cup chopped onion
⅓ cup chopped tomatoes

1 medium clove garlic, minced
½ teaspoon tarragon, crushed
1 can (2 ounces) rolled
   anchovy fillets stuffed with
   capers

Trim fat from meat; place in shallow baking dish (12x8x2 inches). Roast at 350° F. for 1 hour. Spoon off fat. Combine remaining ingredients except anchovies. Pour over meat. Cover with foil; bake 2 hours more or until tender. Spoon off fat. Top roast with anchovies. 6 servings.

❊ Chuck and Potato Bake

3½-pound boned chuck roast
   (about 2-inches thick)
6 medium potatoes (about 2
   pounds), peeled and cut in
   half

2 cans (10½ ounces each)
   condensed cream of
   mushroom soup
1 tablespoon chopped dried
   chives, optional
½ cup grated Cheddar cheese
Paprika

Trim fat from meat; place in large baking pan (13x9x2 inches). Roast at 350° F. for 1 hour; spoon off fat. Arrange potatoes around roast. Combine soup and chives; pour over meat and potatoes. Cover with foil; bake 2 hours more or until meat and potatoes are tender. Sprinkle with cheese and paprika; bake until cheese melts. 6 servings.

❊ Roast Chuck Neopolitan

3½-pound boned chuck roast
   (about 2-inches thick)
2 tablespoons shortening
1 can (10¾ ounces) condensed
   tomato soup

½ cup water
1 cup sliced onion
1 large clove garlic, minced
2 teaspoons oregano, crushed
Generous dash pepper

In large heavy pan, brown meat in shortening. Pour off fat. Stir in remaining ingredients. Cover; cook over low heat 2½ hours or until tender. Spoon off fat. 6 servings.

When preparing herbs you will achieve more flavor from the dry variety by chopping it with a fresh one. For example, try combining fresh parsley and dried tarragon or oregano.

Two popular foods combine in Chuck and Potato Bake with an easy-to-make cheese sauce. Delectable fare for the family or an informal company supper.

Braised Short Ribs with Dumplings

3 pounds short ribs, cut in
   serving-size pieces
2 tablespoons shortening
1 can (10½ ounces) condensed
   cream of celery soup
1 can (10½ ounces) condensed
   onion soup
1 can (16 ounces) tomatoes,
   cut-up

½ cup water
2 tablespoons Worcestershire
2 large cloves garlic, minced
1 medium bay leaf
1 pound carrots, cut in 2-inch
   pieces (about 2 cups)
1½ cups biscuit mix
1 teaspoon ground savory
½ cup milk

Trim excess fat from ribs. In Dutch oven, brown ribs in shortening; pour off fat. Stir in soups, tomatoes, water, Worcestershire, garlic, and bay. Cover; cook over low heat 1 hour 45 minutes. Stir now and then. Add carrots. Cover; cook 1 hour more. Spoon fat off surface, if necessary. Combine biscuit mix and savory; stir in milk. Drop 8 spoonfuls onto boiling stew; cook 10 minutes. Cover; cook 10 minutes more. Serve immediately. 4 servings.

Beef Caribe

4 slices bacon
1½ pounds beef cubes (1½ inch)
1 can (10¾ ounces) condensed
   tomato soup
1 soup can water
1 cup chopped onion
2 medium bay leaves

1 teaspoon paprika
Dash crushed red pepper
4 medium potatoes (about
   1½ pounds), quartered
½ cup pitted ripe olives
1 tablespoon drained capers
1 cup chopped green pepper

In large heavy pan, cook bacon until crisp; remove and crumble. In drippings, brown beef. Add soup, water, onion, bay leaves, paprika, pepper, and bacon. Cover; cook over low heat 1 hour 45 minutes. Stir now and then. Add potatoes, olives, and capers. Cook 45 minutes more or until tender. Add green pepper last 15 minutes. Stir now and then. Remove bay leaves. 4 servings.

Creamed Horseradish Sauce on Cooked Beef

2 eggs, slightly beaten
1 tablespoon milk
Salt and pepper
4 servings sliced cooked beef
2 tablespoons flour
¼ cup fine dry bread crumbs
2 tablespoons butter or margarine

1 can (10½ ounces) condensed
   cream of mushroom soup
¼ cup milk
2 teaspoons prepared
   horseradish
½ teaspoon dried dill leaves,
   crushed

Combine eggs, milk, salt, and pepper. Dip slices of beef in flour, then egg mixture, then crumbs. In skillet, brown beef in butter. Meanwhile, in saucepan, combine remaining ingredients. Heat; stir now and then. Serve sauce over beef. 4 servings.

Tacos

1½ cups chopped cooked beef
½ cup chopped onion
2 large cloves garlic, minced
1 tablespoon chili powder
2 tablespoons salad oil

1 can (10¾ ounces) condensed
   tomato soup
8 tortillas
Grated Cheddar cheese
Shredded lettuce
Chopped avocado

In saucepan, brown beef and cook onion with garlic and chili powder in oil until onion is tender. Add soup. Heat; stir now and then. In skillet, cook one tortilla at a time in hot oil for an instant until it is pliable; remove. Place about ¼ cup meat mixture in center of tortilla; top with cheese, lettuce, and avocado. Fold tortilla in half. Makes 8 tacos.

Ground Beef: Substitute 1 pound ground beef for cooked beef; omit salad oil. Proceed as above. Makes about 10 tacos.

❀ Swedish Chuck Stew

3½-pound boned chuck roast
   (about 2-inches thick)
2 tablespoons shortening
2 cans (10½ ounces each)
   condensed cream of mushroom
   soup
½ cup sour cream

½ cup water
1 teaspoon paprika
Generous dash pepper
1 pound medium carrots, halved
1 pound whole small white
   onions
Cooked wide noodles

Trim fat from meat and cut into 1-inch cubes. In large heavy pan, brown beef in shortening; pour off fat. Add soup, sour cream, water, paprika, and pepper. Cover; cook over low heat 1 hour. Stir now and then. Add vegetables. Cover; cook over low heat 1 hour more or until meat and vegetables are tender. Stir now and then. Serve with noodles. 6 servings.

PORK·VEAL LAMB

Beef may be king, but pork, veal, lamb and variety meats also rank high in the culinary peerage. Readily available, they bring versatility to your table for family meals, holiday celebrations or that particular occasion which calls for something special.

Pork was greatly cherished in early America, not only because it was good eating and nutritious, but because it could be easily preserved—salted, smoked or made into sausages. As our second most popular meat today, it is greatly appreciated for its rich diversity. Fresh or cured, we have chops, roasts, steaks, butts, hocks and tenderloins. There are spareribs, picnics, hams, sausages and the renowned frankfurter.

The texture and taste of veal are entirely different from the meat of mature beef. Because it is so lean, veal should be cooked with the addition of fat, and is generally braised, roasted, stewed, or gently fried. Veal takes to seasoning and combines particularly well with piquant flavors.

Many of our best veal dishes are adaptations from European creations and are excellent party main dishes. For an epicurean meal, feature veal delicately flavored with a superb sauce.

A fine-textured meat with distinctive, appealing flavor, lamb is becoming more appreciated in America. Long esteemed as important fare for special feasts in Europe and the Middle East, it earns its reputation as an elegant entree for company meals.

Lamb has a particular affinity for sauces and stuffings. It is also compatible with a wide range of interesting foods and seasonings which make the various dishes especially attractive. Among the best of them are the delicious stews, casseroles, roasts, patties and increasingly popular skewered shish kabobs.

Plan a cosy oven supper for a wintry eve—and serve this homey casserole. Before you put in the meat dish, bake cinnamon-rosy apples for dessert.

Meat 'n Biscuit Bake

1½ cups cubed cooked beef, lamb, pork, or veal
¼ teaspoon oregano, crushed
2 tablespoons butter or margarine
1 can (10½ ounces) condensed golden mushroom soup
½ cup water

½ cup chopped canned tomatoes
1 cup cooked cut green beans
1 cup biscuit mix
2 tablespoons grated Parmesan cheese

In saucepan, brown meat with oregano in butter. Stir in soup, ¼ cup water, tomatoes, and beans. Pour into 1½-quart casserole. Bake at 450°F. for 10 minutes. Meanwhile, combine biscuit mix and ¼ cup water; mix as directed on package. Roll into 8-inch square; sprinkle with cheese. Roll up jelly-roll fashion; cut into 8 slices. Place biscuits around edge. Bake 15 minutes more or until browned. 4 servings.

❋ Country-Fried Pork Chops

4 pork chops (about 1 pound)
1 can (2 ounces) sliced mushrooms, drained
1 tablespoon shortening
1 can (10½ ounces) condensed cream of celery soup

½ cup water
¼ teaspoon leaf thyme, crushed
6 whole small white onions
1 cup sliced carrots

In skillet, brown chops and mushrooms in shortening; pour off fat. Stir in soup, water, and thyme. Add onions and carrots. Cover; cook over low heat 45 minutes or until tender. Stir now and then. 3 to 4 servings.

Texas Pork Chops

1 can (11 ounces) condensed chili beef soup
1 cup cooked rice
2 tablespoons finely chopped green pepper
2 tablespoons sliced ripe olives

4 pork chops (about 1½ pounds), ¾-inch thick
1 can (1 pound) tomatoes
1 medium onion, sliced
1 medium clove garlic, minced

Combine ¼ cup soup, rice, green pepper, and olives. Trim excess fat from chops. Slit each chop from outer edge toward bone making a pocket; stuff with rice mixture. Fasten with toothpicks. In skillet, brown chops; pour off fat. Add remaining ingredients. Cover; cook over low heat 1¼ hours. Stir now and then breaking up tomatoes. Uncover; cook to desired consistency. 4 servings.

❋ Pork Chops Charcutiere

6 pork chops (about 1½ pounds)
1 can (10½ ounces) condensed
    golden mushroom soup
⅓ cup water
⅓ cup chopped onion

2 teaspoons prepared mustard
2 tablespoons sweet or dill
    gherkin pickles,
    cut in strips

In skillet, brown chops; pour off fat. Add soup, water, onion, and mustard. Cover; cook over low heat 45 minutes or until tender. Stir now and then. Add pickles last 5 minutes. 4 servings.

❋ Pork Chops a l'Orange

8 rib pork chops (about 2
    pounds)
Pepper
2 cans (10½ ounces each)
    condensed cream of chicken
    soup

1 cup fresh orange juice
½ cup diagonally sliced celery
4 tablespoons coarsely chopped
    cashews
Generous dash ground cloves
8 fresh orange slices, cut in
    half

Use 1 large skillet or prepare in 2 skillets (about 10 inch); prepare by dividing ingredients equally. Brown chops; season with pepper. Pour off fat. Stir in remaining ingredients except orange. Cover; cook over low heat 40 minutes. Stir now and then. Add orange slices. Cover; cook over low heat 5 minutes more or until meat is tender. 6 servings.

❋ Ham 'n Turkey Casserole

2 cups ham strips
1 teaspoon poultry seasoning
1 tablespoon butter or margarine
2 cans (10½ ounces each)
    condensed cream of celery
    soup
⅔ cup milk
2 cups cubed cooked turkey

1 can (1 pound) small whole
    white onions, drained
1 package (10 ounces) frozen
    peas, cooked and drained
2 packages (8 ounces each)
    refrigerated crescent rolls
1 package (8 ounces) sliced
    process cheese or ½ cup
    shredded Cheddar cheese

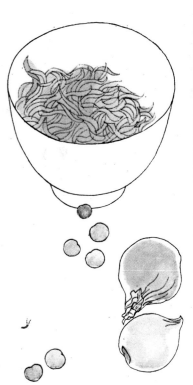

In saucepan, brown ham with poultry seasoning in butter. In shallow baking dish (13x9x2 inches), combine ham with remaining ingredients except rolls and cheese. Bake at 400°F. for 20 minutes or until hot. Meanwhile, cut cheese slices diagonally in half. Separate rolls. Top each roll with cheese triangle. Roll up as directed on package. Stir hot casserole; top with rolls. Bake 15 to 20 minutes more or until rolls are done. 8 servings.

Stuffed Chops and Yams

1 cup diced apple
⅓ cup chopped celery
¼ cup raisins
½ teaspoon paprika
2 tablespoons butter
    or margarine
4 thick pork chops
    (about 1½ pounds)

1 can (10½ ounces)
    condensed golden mushroom
    soup
½ cup sour cream
¼ cup water
1 can (1 pound) sweet potatoes,
    drained

Look for well-marbled and finely textured meat in pork chops. The choices are: loin (with a T-shaped bone), rib (with rib bone), butterfly (boneless) and smoked (with ham-like flavor).

In saucepan, cook apple, celery, raisins, and ¼ teaspoon paprika in butter until celery is tender. Trim excess fat from chops. Slit each chop from outer edge toward the bone making a pocket; stuff with apple mixture; fasten with skewers or toothpicks. In skillet, brown chops; pour off fat. Stir in soup, sour cream, water, and remaining paprika. Cover; cook over low heat 1 hour 20 minutes or until tender. Add potatoes; heat 10 minutes more. Stir now and then. 4 servings.

Chops 'n Cabbage Skillet

6 pork chops (about 1½ pounds)
½ cup chopped onion
2 tablespoons shortening
1 can (10½ ounces) condensed
    cream of celery soup

½ cup water
1 teaspoon caraway seed
Generous dash pepper
4 cabbage wedges, 2 inches
    wide (about 1 pound)

In skillet, brown chops and onion in shortening; pour off fat. Stir in soup, water, caraway, and pepper. Arrange cabbage on top of chops. Cover; cook over low heat 1 hour. Stir now and then. 4 servings.

Saucy Pork Chops

4 pork chops (about 1 pound)
Salt and pepper
4 onion slices

4 green pepper rings
1 can (10¾ ounces)
    condensed tomato soup

In skillet, brown chops on both sides; pour off fat. Sprinkle chops with seasonings; place slice of onion and pepper ring on each; pour soup over. Cover; cook over low heat for 45 minutes or until tender. Stir now and then. 3 to 4 servings.

Flavorful Stuffed Chops and Yams *with a mushroom sauce becomes a superb supper. Cook and serve in the same attractive skillet.*

Pork with Shrimp

1 pound boneless loin of pork,
  cut in very thin strips
2 tablespoons salad oil
1 can (10¾ ounces) condensed
  tomato soup
1 pound medium shrimp (about
  18), cleaned and cut in half
  lengthwise

¼ cup water
2 tablespoons finely chopped
  chutney
2 tablespoons chopped green
  pepper
1 tablespoon lemon juice
Generous dash coriander

In skillet, brown pork in oil. Add remaining ingredients. Cover; cook over low heat 10 minutes or until pork and shrimp are done. Stir now and then. Serve with hot fluffy rice. 6 servings.

Baked Spareribs with Sauerkraut

4 pounds spareribs, cut in
  serving-size pieces
Pepper
1 can (10½ ounces) condensed
  onion soup

1 can (1 pound 11 ounces)
  sauerkraut
1½ cups shredded apple
1 teaspoon caraway

Sprinkle spareribs with pepper; arrange fat side up in shallow baking pan (14x10 x2 inches). Bake at 325°F. for 1½ hours turning once. Remove ribs; pour off fat. Combine remaining ingredients in pan; top with ribs. Bake 1½ hours more. 4 servings.

Roast Pork Party-Style

3-pound loin of pork
6 slices onion
3 slices apple, cut in half
  (¼-inch thick)
¼ teaspoon sage

1 can (10½ ounces) condensed
  cream of chicken soup
¼ cup Madeira or Sherry
⅓ to ½ cup water

Make 6 slits almost to bone in pork loin. Place a slice of onion and ½ slice apple in each slit. Rub roast with sage. Tie securely. Roast fat side up at 325°F. for 2 hours. Pour off fat. Combine soup and Madeira; pour over meat. Roast 30 minutes more or until done, basting often with soup (total roasting time takes 35 to 40 minutes per pound or 170°F. on meat thermometer). Remove meat from pan. On top of range, in roasting pan, add water to soup. Heat, stirring to loosen browned bits. Serve with roast. 4 to 6 servings.

Veal Chops Roma

6 veal chops (about 1½ pounds)
1 medium clove garlic, minced
½ teaspoon oregano, crushed
3 tablespoons butter or margarine

1 can (10¾ ounces) condensed
   tomato soup
½ cup sliced onion
1 cup green pepper strips
½ cup sliced ripe olives

In skillet, brown chops and cook garlic with oregano in butter. Add soup and onion. Cover; cook over low heat 30 minutes. Add pepper and olives. Cook 15 minutes more or until done. Stir now and then. 4 servings.

❋ Veal Scallopine Marsala

1½ pounds thinly sliced veal
   tenders
¼ cup butter or margarine
¼ cup Marsala wine

1 can (10½ ounces) condensed
   beef broth
1 tablespoon flour

Cut veal into 3-inch pieces; pound. In skillet, brown veal in butter. Add wine. Bring to boil; stir to loosen browned bits. Gradually blend broth into flour until smooth. Slowly stir into wine. Cook, stirring until thickened. 6 servings.

Veal Birds with Polenta

1½ pounds thinly sliced veal
   cutlet
6 thin slices proscuitto (Italian
   ham)
2 slices (about 3 ounces) Mozzarella cheese, cut in 6 pieces
2 tablespoons butter or margarine
2 tablespoons chopped onion

1 medium clove garlic, minced
1 can (10½ ounces) condensed
   cream of mushroom soup
⅓ cup milk
4 cups water
1 cup cornmeal
1 teaspoon salt

Once upon a time a luxurious Italian dish was roasted small birds and polenta. Over the years thin slices of meat, stuffed and rolled up, became known as "poor men's birds" which are now regal fare.

Cut veal into 6 pieces (about 6x4 inches); pound. Place 1 slice proscuitto on each piece veal; top with cheese. Roll up; fasten with toothpicks. In skillet, brown roll-ups in butter; push to side and cook onion with garlic until tender. Stir in soup and milk. Cover; cook over low heat 45 minutes or until tender. Stir now and then. Meanwhile, mix 1 cup water, cornmeal, and salt; pour into 3 cups boiling water, stirring constantly. Cook until thickened, stirring often. Cover; cook over low heat for 25 minutes. Spoon mush around edge of platter; arrange roll-ups in center. 6 servings.

Cranberry Glazed Ham with Sauce

5-pound canned ham
¾ cup jellied cranberry sauce
1 can (10½ ounces) condensed
   consomme

½ cup applesauce
1 tablespoon cornstarch
1 teaspoon lemon juice
Generous dash allspice

In shallow baking pan, bake ham at 325°F. for 1 hour. Pour off fat. Score; spread ¼ cup cranberry sauce over top. Bake 30 minutes more (15 minutes per pound or 130°F. on meat thermometer). Remove to platter. In baking pan, combine remaining ingredients. Cook, stirring constantly until thickened. Pour some sauce over ham; serve remainder. 8 to 10 servings.

Veal Roast South Pacific

¼ cup softened butter or
   margarine
2 to 3 teaspoons curry powder
1 large clove garlic, minced
3-pound veal roast (rump)

1 can (10½ ounces) condensed
   cream of celery soup
½ cup sour cream
⅓ cup water
½ cup drained pineapple
   tidbits

Combine butter, curry, and garlic. Spread on top and sides of veal. Roast at 325° F. for 2 hours or until done (35 to 40 minutes per pound or 170° F. on meat thermometer). Remove veal from pan. Pour off fat, saving drippings. On top of range, in roasting pan, blend soup and sour cream into drippings. Add water and pineapple. Heat, stirring to loosen browned bits. Serve with roast. 6 servings.

Creamed Sweetbreads Olivero

1 pound sweetbreads
½ cup sliced onion
1 medium clove garlic, minced
2 tablespoons butter or margarine
1 can (10½ ounces) condensed
   cream of mushroom soup

⅓ cup milk
⅓ cup chopped canned
   tomatoes
¼ cup sliced stuffed olives
Cooked rice

For a party, precook sweetbreads (lamb, veal or beef); then cube and brown them with seasonings before the guests arrive. Add remaining prepared ingredients minutes before serving.

In saucepan, combine 1 quart water, 1 teaspoon salt, and 1 tablespoon lemon juice. Bring to a boil. Add sweetbreads. Cover; cook over low heat 20 minutes. Drain; remove membrane. Cut sweetbreads into cubes. In saucepan, brown sweetbreads and cook onion and garlic in butter until onion is tender. Add soup, milk, tomatoes, and olives. Heat; stir now and then. Serve over rice. 4 servings.

Planning to feature ham for a buffet party? Everyday canned ham becomes an elegant entree as Cranberry Glazed Ham.

❋ Sunday Best Veal Rolls

1 cup chopped onion
¼ cup butter or margarine
½ cup chopped parsley
1½ pounds veal cutlet, ¼-inch
    thick

1 can (10½ ounces) condensed
    cream of celery soup
1 teaspoon grated lemon rind
Whipped potatoes
Frosted grapes
Lemon wedges

In skillet, cook onion in 2 tablespoons butter until tender; add parsley. Cut veal into 6 pieces (about 6x4 inches); pound. Place about 1 tablespoon onion mixture on each piece of veal; roll up and fasten with toothpicks or skewers. In same skillet, brown veal in remaining butter. Add soup. Cover; cook over low heat 45 minutes or until tender. Stir now and then. Add rind. Serve with potatoes; garnish with grapes and lemon. 4 to 6 servings.

❋ Veal Saltimbocca

8 thin slices veal cutlet
    (about 1½ pounds)
¼ teaspoon sage
8 thin slices prosciutto ham
    (about 4 ounces)
2 tablespoons butter or margarine

½ cup Chablis or other dry
    white wine
1 can (10½ ounces)
    condensed golden mushroom
    soup
½ cup water

Pound veal; rub with sage. Place slice of ham on each piece; fasten with toothpicks. In skillet, brown veal side down in butter. Do not turn. Add wine; bring to boil. Stir to loosen browned bits. Simmer a few minutes. Stir in soup and water; heat. 6 servings.

This famous French dish is a rich ragout or stew made with veal or chicken, mushrooms and onions. It is named for its creamy white sauce.

❋ Blanquette de Veau

1 can (10½ ounces) condensed
    chicken broth
2 pounds veal cubes
    (about 1½ inches)
2 tablespoons chopped parsley
1 small clove garlic, minced
1 teaspoon lemon juice
½ teaspoon thyme, crushed

Generous dash ground cloves
1 pound (about 16) small
    whole white onions
2 cups small fresh mushroom
    caps (about ½ pound)
¾ cup light cream
3 tablespoons flour
Cooked rice

In skillet, combine broth, veal, parsley, garlic, lemon juice, thyme, and cloves. Cover; cook over low heat 1 hour. Stir now and then. Add onions and mushrooms. Cook 30 minutes more or until meat and vegetables are tender. Gradually blend cream into flour until smooth; slowly stir into sauce. Cook, stirring until thickened. Serve with rice. 6 servings.

❋ Veal Chasseur

1 pound thinly sliced veal, cut
    into serving-size pieces
2 tablespoons butter or margarine
1 can (10½ ounces) condensed
    golden mushroom soup
¼ cup water

½ cup chopped canned
    tomatoes
4 small whole white onions
2 tablespoons white wine
¼ teaspoon chervil

Pound veal with meat hammer or edge of heavy saucer. In skillet, brown veal in butter; add remaining ingredients. Cover; cook over low heat 20 minutes or until tender. Stir now and then. 4 servings.

Lamb Breast, Sausage Stuffing

1 pound sausage
1 cup chopped celery
1 large clove garlic, minced
1 package (8 ounces) herb-
    seasoned stuffing mix
1 can (10½ ounces) condensed
    onion soup

2 breasts of lamb with pocket
    for stuffing (about 2 pounds
    each)
2 teaspoons rosemary, crushed
1 can (10½ ounces)
    condensed cream of
    mushroom soup
⅓ cup water
¼ cup chopped chutney

In skillet, brown sausage and cook celery with garlic. Add stuffing mix and 1 cup onion soup. Toss lightly. Spoon ½ stuffing into each breast; fasten with skewers. Rub each breast with 1 teaspoon rosemary. Roast at 325°F. for 1 hour 15 minutes or until done (35 to 40 minutes per pound or 175°F. on meat thermometer). Remove meat from pan. Pour off fat, saving drippings. On top of range, in roasting pan, add mushroom soup, water, chutney, and remaining onion soup. Heat, stirring to loosen browned bits. Serve with roast. 6 servings.

Lamb 'n Rice Skillet

1½ pounds lamb cubes (about
    1 inch), well-trimmed
2 tablespoons shortening
1 can (10½ ounces) condensed
    beef broth
½ cup sliced onion

1 medium clove garlic, minced
¼ teaspoon thyme, crushed
⅔ cup raw regular rice
1 package (10 ounces)
    frozen peas
¼ cup cashews

In skillet, brown lamb in shortening; pour off fat. Add broth, onion, garlic, and thyme. Cover; cook over low heat 30 minutes. Add rice and peas. Cover; cook 25 to 30 minutes more or until lamb and rice are tender. Stir now and then. Add cashews. 4 servings.

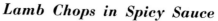

Lamb Chops in Spicy Sauce

4 shoulder lamb chops (about
   1½ pounds), trimmed
½ cup cubed ham
1 tablespoon shortening
1 can (10¾ ounces) condensed
   tomato soup

½ cup sliced onion
¼ cup water
⅛ teaspoon nutmeg
Generous dash mace, optional
Buttered noodles

In skillet, brown chops and ham in shortening; pour off fat. Add remaining ingredients except noodles. Cover; cook over low heat 45 minutes or until chops are tender. Stir now and then. Serve with noodles. 4 servings.

Quick Cutlets Italiano

½ cup chopped onion
1 large clove garlic, minced
¼ teaspoon oregano, crushed
⅛ teaspoon thyme, crushed
2 tablespoons butter or margarine
1 can (10¾ ounces) condensed
   tomato soup
½ cup water

1 can (12 ounces) luncheon
   meat, cut in 8 slices
1 egg, slightly beaten
½ cup bread crumbs
2 tablespoons shortening
2 slices (3 ounces)
   Mozzarella cheese
Grated Parmesan cheese

In saucepan, cook onion with garlic, oregano, and thyme in butter until tender. Stir in soup and water; cook over low heat 15 minutes. Stir now and then. Meanwhile, dip luncheon meat slices in egg, then in bread crumbs. In skillet, brown meat on one side in shortening; turn and pour sauce over. Top with Mozzarella; sprinkle with Parmesan. Cover until cheese melts (about 3 minutes). 4 servings.

Lamb Indienne

1½ pounds lamb cubes
   (about 1½ inches)
2 tablespoons shortening
1 can (10½ ounces) condensed
   cream of chicken soup
½ cup sliced onion
½ cup water

1 large clove garlic, minced
1 tablespoon curry powder
Dash ground cardamon
Dash ground coriander
1 cup diced apple
3 cups cooked rice

In large heavy pan, brown lamb in shortening; pour off fat. Add soup, onion, water, garlic, and seasonings. Cover; cook over low heat 1½ hours or until tender. Stir now and then. Add apple the last 5 minutes. Serve with rice. Garnish with chopped chutney, toasted coconut, raisins. 4 servings.

A treasured foreign food is Lamb Indienne, *a subtly seasoned curried dish. Serve over rice. Let guests help themselves to the attractive and toothsome tidbits for garnish.*

Canadian Bacon and Yam Bake

1 can (about 13 ounces)
    pineapple chunks
1 cup green pepper strips (2x1/4")
2 tablespoons butter or margarine
1 can (10½ ounces) condensed
    beef broth
2 tablespoons cornstarch

2 tablespoons honey
2 teaspoons lemon juice
½ teaspoon dry mustard
1 can (16 ounces) sweet potatoes,
    drained
1 pound Canadian bacon, cut into
    8 slices

Drain pineapple reserving ⅓ cup syrup. In saucepan, cook green pepper in butter until tender. Stir in soup, reserved pineapple syrup, cornstarch, honey, lemon juice, and mustard. Cook, stirring constantly until thickened. In 1½-quart casserole, arrange alternate layers of potatoes, bacon, pineapple, and sauce. Cover; bake at 350°F. for 45 minutes. 4 servings.

✻ Frankfurter Crown Casserole

2 slices bacon
½ cup chopped onion
1 can (10½ ounces) condensed
    cream of mushroom soup
½ cup water
½ teaspoon salt

Dash pepper
3 cups sliced cooked potatoes
1 cup cooked cut green beans
½ pound frankfurters, split
    and cut in half

In skillet, cook bacon. Remove and crumble. Cook onion in drippings until tender. Stir in soup, water, salt, and pepper; add potatoes and green beans. Pour into 1½-quart casserole. Stand frankfurters around edge of casserole. Bake at 350°F. for 30 minutes. Garnish with bacon. 3 to 4 servings.

Sausage 'n Noodles Napoli

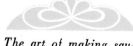

The art of making sausages is one of the world's oldest ways of preparing meats. The word derives from the Latin for salt. Many of our varieties came from Europe but early colonists excelled in sausage making.

½ pound sausage links
½ pound Italian sausage, cut in
    1-inch pieces
1 can (10½ ounces) condensed
    onion soup
1 can (about 4 ounces) sliced
    mushrooms, drained

½ cup chopped celery
½ cup chopped canned
    tomatoes
2 cups cooked fine egg noodles
1 package (10 ounces) frozen
    peas, cooked and drained

In skillet, brown sausages; pour off fat. Add soup, mushrooms, celery, and tomatoes. Cover; cook over low heat 10 minutes. Add noodles and peas. Cook 10 minutes more. Stir now and then. 4 servings.

Skillet Frankaroni

6 frankfurters, slashed
½ cup chopped green pepper
½ cup chopped onion
1 teaspoon chili powder
¼ cup butter or margarine
1 can (10¾ ounces) condensed
    Cheddar cheese soup

½ cup water
2 cups cooked elbow macaroni
1 package (9 ounces) frozen
    cut green beans, cooked and
    drained

In skillet, brown frankfurters and cook pepper and onion with chili powder in butter until tender. Stir in soup and water. Add macaroni and beans. Heat; stir now and then. 3 to 4 servings.

Sausage-Apple Bake

1 pound bulk sausage
1 cup shredded apple
⅓ cup fine dry bread crumbs
¼ cup finely chopped onion
1 egg, slightly beaten
Generous dash pepper
2 cans (10½ ounces each)
    condensed beef broth

¼ cup water
1½ cups sliced carrots
    (½-inch thick)
⅛ teaspoon mace
1 cup raw regular rice
3 apple slices (½-inch thick),
    cut in half

Combine sausage, apple, crumbs, onion, egg, and pepper; mix thoroughly. Shape into 16 meatballs. In oven-proof skillet, brown meatballs; pour off fat. Stir in broth, water, carrots, and mace. Bring to boil; stir in rice. Cover; bake at 450°F. for 15 minutes. Stir; arrange apple pieces between meatballs. Cover; bake 10 minutes more or until rice is tender. Stir. 4 servings.

Bologna Bundles

1 can (11½ ounces) condensed
    bean with bacon soup
⅓ cup chopped dill pickle
1 tablespoon grated onion

1 pound bologna, cut into
    ¼-inch thick slices
½ cup shredded Cheddar
    cheese
Paprika

Combine soup, pickle, and onion; place equal amounts soup mixture on each slice bologna. Fold over; fasten with toothpicks or skewers. Arrange in shallow baking dish (12x8x2 inches). Bake at 350°F. for 20 minutes. Sprinkle with cheese and paprika; bake 10 minutes more. 4 servings.

SEAFOOD

The world of seafood is fascinating to contemplate and pleasurable to explore. And our country is blessed with a wide variety of foods from the sea. Available fresh, frozen or canned, we can offer seafood to our family and friends as a welcome change of pace. In one form or another, fish and shellfish can make a menu memorable.

Without these denizens of the sea, the American colonists might not have survived. In those early days, and for many decades thereafter, our forefathers were limited to seafood in season or those which had been preserved. Generally they were acquainted with only those in their own or nearby locales. However, this did not hinder the creation of many superb seafood dishes which have become classics of the American table.

Among these excellent regional specialties are New England's seafood and clam chowders, oyster stew, codfish cakes and fried clams. In the Middle Atlantic states cooks prepare native crabs and oysters in many ways and are fond of baked stuffed rockfish and seafood pies. In the South there are such famous delights as baked red snapper, Creole gumbo, jambalaya and stuffed crabs. Westerners are fond of their salmon steaks, Dungeness crabs and delectable cioppino.

Fortunately, everyone can now enjoy at least some of these regional specialties and many other seafood dishes. Modern progress in canning, freezing and transportation makes much of the nation's seafood bounty available everywhere and at any time of the year.

Cooking seafood is not difficult, just remember that it should not be overcooked or the precious juices will be lost.

The hostess who serves her guests seafood may also take pleasure in offering them a culinary treat that is low in calories and rich in nutritive value.

❊ *Fish Bonne Femme*

1½ pounds fillet of sole or
   flounder
1 cup sliced fresh mushrooms
   (about ¼ pound)
2 tablespoons finely chopped
   onion
2 tablespoons chopped parsley

½ cup Chablis or other dry
   white wine
1 can (10½ ounces)
   condensed cream of celery
   soup
¼ cup heavy cream, whipped

In skillet, place sole on bottom; top with mushrooms, onion, and parsley. Add wine. Cover; cook over low heat 10 minutes. Carefully transfer fish and garnish to oven-proof platter. Stir soup into ¼ cup of the remaining liquid; heat. Fold in whipped cream. Pour over fish. Place under broiler until lightly browned. 6 servings.

Fillet of Sole Veronique: Omit mushrooms, onion, and parsley from above recipe. Substitute 1 cup seedless white grapes.

❊ *Perfect Tuna Casserole*

1 can (10½ ounces) condensed
   cream of celery or mushroom
   soup
¼ cup milk
1 can (7 ounces) tuna, drained
   and flaked

2 hard-cooked eggs, sliced
1 cup cooked peas
½ cup slightly crumbled
   potato chips

In 1-quart casserole, blend soup and milk; stir in tuna, eggs, and peas. Bake at 350°F. for 25 minutes. Top with chips; bake 5 minutes more or until hot. 3 to 4 servings.

Easy Tuna Rice

⅓ cup chopped onion
2 tablespoons butter or margarine
1 can (10½ ounces) condensed
   chicken broth
1 cup quick cooking rice,
   uncooked

¼ cup sliced water chestnuts
1 teaspoon soy sauce
1 can (7 ounces) tuna, drained
   and flaked
1 cup cooked Italian green
   beans

In saucepan, cook onion in butter until tender. Add broth, rice, chestnuts, and soy. Bring to a boil. Cover; cook over low heat about 5 minutes or until all liquid is absorbed. Add tuna and beans; heat. Serve with additional soy. 3 to 4 servings.

Favorite Curried Tuna

1/4 cup sliced green onions
1 teaspoon curry powder
2 tablespoons butter or margarine
1 can (10½ ounces) condensed
  cream of chicken soup
1/3 cup milk

½ cup chopped unpeeled apple
1/4 cup toasted slivered
  almonds
1 can (7 ounces) tuna,
  drained and flaked
3 or 4 patty shells

In saucepan, cook onions with curry in butter until tender. Stir in remaining ingredients except patty shells. Heat; stir now and then. Serve in patty shells. 3 to 4 servings.

✳ Famous Seafood Stew

2 lobster tails (about ½ pound)
1 cup sliced onion
1 medium clove garlic, minced
2 tablespoons butter or margarine
1 can (10¾ ounces) condensed
  clam chowder (Manhattan style)
1 can (10½ ounces) condensed
  New England clam chowder

½ cup water
1/4 cup Chablis or other dry
  white wine
1 pound scallops
2 tablespoons chopped parsley
1 pound white fish, cut in
  2-inch pieces

Remove lobster meat from shells; cut up. In large pan, cook onion with garlic in butter until tender. Add remaining ingredients except fish. Cook over low heat 5 minutes; add fish. Cook 5 minutes more or until fish is done. Stir now and then. 8 servings. If desired, before serving stew, place in each bowl a slice of Italian bread fixed this way. (Spread with butter, sprinkle with crushed dill; bake at 450° F. for 10 minutes).

Gourmet Shrimp

1/4 cup chopped onion
2 tablespoons chopped parsley
2 tablespoons chopped shallots
2 tablespoons butter or margarine
2 pounds shrimp, shelled and
  deveined

1 can (10½ ounces) condensed
  cream of mushroom soup
½ cup chopped canned tomatoes
1/4 cup cognac

In skillet, cook onion, parsley, and shallots in butter until onion is tender. Add remaining ingredients except cognac. Cover; cook over low heat 10 minutes. Stir now and then. Carefully heat cognac; set it aflame, and pour over shrimp mixture. 6 servings.

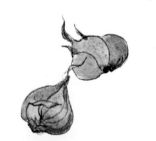

❋ Crab Louis

1 can (10½ ounces) condensed
   cream of celery soup
½ cup chili sauce
¼ cup mayonnaise
2 tablespoons minced onion
Generous dash pepper

¼ cup heavy cream, whipped
4 cups (about 1½ pounds)
   crab meat
Hard-cooked egg, cut in wedges
Tomatoes, cut in wedges

Blend soup, chili, mayonnaise, onion, and pepper; fold in whipped cream. Add crab; chill. Place crab on bed of lettuce. Garnish with egg and tomato. 6 servings.

Swordfish with Cucumber Sauce

2 teaspoons anchovy paste
6 tablespoons softened
   butter or margarine
6 swordfish steaks
   (about 1½ pounds)
1 cup diced cucumber
½ teaspoon dried dill leaves,
   crushed

2 tablespoons butter
   or margarine
1 can (10½ ounces)
   condensed cream of
   mushroom soup
⅓ cup sour cream

Cream anchovy paste and softened butter; spread on steaks. Broil 4 inches from heat for 5 minutes on each side or until fish flakes easily. Meanwhile, in saucepan, cook cucumber with dill in butter until tender. Add soup and sour cream. Heat; stir now and then. Serve over fish. 6 servings.

Little Salmon Loaves with Mushroom Sauce

2 cans (7½ ounces each)
   salmon, drained and flaked
1 can (10½ ounces) condensed
   cream of mushroom soup
1 egg, slightly beaten
½ cup finely chopped onion
¼ cup fine dry bread crumbs

2 teaspoons prepared
   horseradish
½ teaspoon prepared mustard
¼ cup sour cream
2 tablespoons water
¼ cup chopped canned
   tomatoes
2 teaspoons chopped chives

In bowl, combine salmon, ¼ cup soup, egg, onion, crumbs, horseradish, and mustard. Mix well. Pack into well-buttered individual molds or custard cups (6-ounce size). Bake at 350°F. for 20 minutes. Unmold. Meanwhile, combine remaining ingredients. Heat; stir now and then. Serve over salmon. 4 servings.

Two prized fruits of the sea with inventive sauces, Crab Louis
and Swordfish with Cucumber Sauce.

Lobster Cantonese

½ pound ground pork
2 medium cloves garlic, minced
¼ cup vegetable oil
1½ pounds raw lobster, cut in
   bite-size pieces
1 can (10½ ounces) condensed
   chicken broth
1 soup can water

½ cup diagonally sliced
   green onions
2 tablespoons soy sauce
Generous dash pepper
3 tablespoons cornstarch
¼ cup water
1 egg, slightly beaten

In skillet, cook pork and garlic in oil until done; stir. Add lobster, soup, water, onions, soy, and pepper. Cook over low heat 2 to 3 minutes or until lobster is done. Mix cornstarch and ¼ cup water; gradually add to sauce. Cook, stirring until thickened. Stir egg into sauce. 6 servings.

Crab au Gratin

There are numerous fine foods to serve in attractive individual sea shells or baking dishes. Two of them are Crab au Gratin and Coquille St. Jacques, superb luncheon fare.

1 cup sliced mushrooms
   (about ¼ pound)
¼ cup chopped onion
¼ teaspoon marjoram, crushed
2 tablespoons butter or margarine
1 can (10½ ounces) condensed
   cream of celery soup

1 tablespoon Sherry
1 can (7 ounces) crab,
   drained and flaked
¼ cup shredded Swiss cheese
Paprika

In saucepan, brown mushrooms and cook onion with marjoram in butter until tender. Stir in soup, Sherry, and crab. Heat; stir now and then. Spoon into 4 individual seashells or baking dishes. Sprinkle with cheese and paprika. Broil until cheese melts. 4 servings.

❋ Broiled Lobster Tails au Gratin
Pictured on back cover

4 lobster tails (about 2 pounds)
½ cup sliced green onions
¼ teaspoon chervil, crushed
2 tablespoons butter or margarine

1 can (10½ ounces)
   condensed cream of
   mushroom soup
¼ cup sour cream
½ cup shredded Cheddar
   cheese

Cook lobster tails in boiling water for 10 minutes or until done. Remove meat (keeping shells intact); cut in 1-inch pieces. In saucepan, cook onion with chervil in butter until tender. Add soup, sour cream, and lobster. Heat; stir now and then. Spoon lobster mixture into shells. Top with cheese. Broil 4 to 5 inches from heat until cheese melts. 4 servings.

❋ Coquille St. Jacques

1½ pounds scallops
2 cups sliced mushrooms
  (about ½ pound)
2 tablespoons sliced green
  onions
¼ cup butter or margarine

1 can (10½ ounces) condensed
  cream of celery soup
⅓ cup Chablis or other dry
  white wine
2 tablespoons chopped parsley
¼ cup buttered bread crumbs

In saucepan, cook scallops in water over low heat for 10 minutes; drain well.
Meanwhile, in saucepan, cook mushrooms and green onions in butter until tender.
Add soup, wine, parsley, and scallops. Heat; stir now and then. Spoon into 6
individual baking dishes. Top with crumbs. Place under broiler until lightly
browned. 6 servings.

Lobster Continental on Rice

1 whole chicken breast (about
  ¾ pound), split, skinned, and
  boned
⅛ teaspoon tarragon, crushed
2 tablespoons butter or margarine
2 cans (10¾ ounces each)
  condensed Cheddar cheese soup
⅔ cup milk

⅓ cup Sherry
2 cups cubed cooked lobster
1 package (9 ounces) frozen
  artichokes, cooked and
  drained
½ cup chopped tomatoes
3 cups cooked rice
¼ cup chopped watercress

Cut chicken into strips. In skillet, brown chicken with tarragon in butter. Stir in
soup, milk, and Sherry. Add lobster, artichokes, and tomatoes. Heat; stir now and
then. Meanwhile, combine rice and watercress. Serve lobster mixture over rice. 6
servings.

Tempting Seafood Casserole

½ cup chopped celery
¼ cup chopped onion
2 tablespoons chopped green
  pepper
2 tablespoons butter or margarine
1 can (10½ ounces) condensed
  cream of mushroom soup

¼ cup water
2 cups diced cooked lobster or
  shrimp
1 teaspoon lemon juice
½ cup shredded mild
  process cheese
2 tablespoons buttered bread
  crumbs

In saucepan, cook celery, onion, and pepper in butter until tender. Add remaining ingredients except cheese and crumbs. Pour into 1-quart casserole. Bake at
350°F. for 25 minutes; stir. Top with cheese and crumbs. Bake 5 minutes more
or until hot. 4 servings.

❈ Flounder Florentine

¼ cup chopped onion
⅛ teaspoon rosemary, crushed
2 tablespoons butter or margarine
1 package (9½ ounces) frozen
    chopped spinach, cooked and
    well-drained
½ cup cooked rice
¼ cup chopped toasted almonds

1 tablespoon lemon juice
6 fillets of flounder (about
    1½ pounds)
1 can (10½ ounces) condensed
    cream of mushroom soup
⅓ cup water
Paprika

In saucepan, cook onion with rosemary in butter until tender. Add spinach, rice, almonds, and lemon juice. Heat; stir now and then. Place ¼ cup mixture on each fish fillet. Roll; secure with toothpicks. Arrange in shallow baking dish (10x6x2 inches). Bake at 350°F. for 20 minutes. Meanwhile, blend soup and water; pour over fish, stirring around sides. Bake 15 minutes more or until done. Stir sauce before serving. Sprinkle with paprika. 6 servings.

A welcome change of pace for fish fanciers, Flounder Florentine has a stuffing of almonds, spinach and rice. Generously ladled over all, creamy mushroom sauce

Cioppino

½ cup chopped green pepper
½ cup chopped onion
2 medium cloves garlic, minced
¼ teaspoon oregano, crushed
Generous dash crushed leaf thyme
¼ cup olive oil
2 cans (10¾ ounces each) condensed tomato soup
1 cup water

½ cup Sauterne or other dry white wine
1 pound shrimp, shelled and deveined
2 lobster tails (½ pound), cracked
2 tablespoons chopped parsley
1 medium bay leaf
1 pound haddock fillet, cut in 2-inch pieces

In large pan, cook green pepper, onion, garlic, oregano, and thyme in oil until vegetables are tender. Add remaining ingredients except haddock. Cook over low heat 10 minutes. Add haddock; cook 10 minutes more. Stir gently now and then. 6 to 8 servings.

POULTRY

Our domesticated fowl—chicken, turkey, duckling and Rock Cornish hens—rate high as choice entrees for entertaining. They have universal appeal, exceptional flavor and versatility. Once luxury fare, poultry is now a favorite for all seasons and all occasions.

It was Henry IV of France who promised his people a chicken in every pot, or *poule au pot,* and who did a great deal to popularize the bird. But the globe-trotting chicken, native to Southeast Asia, traversed the world to become important in every cuisine.

Early Americans took pride in presenting chicken for company dinners, particularly on Sunday. They served it fried, smothered, barbecued, baked, roasted, creamed, made into pie, shortcake, fricassee, *a la* King or Brunswick stew. Every table of any epicurian worth featured one or more kinds of chicken.

Moderate in calories and high in protein, chicken comes fresh, frozen or canned. Contributing greatly to its ease of preparation are the readily available chicken parts which do not require much handling before cooking.

Turkey, a gift of the New World to the Old, has been associated traditionally with winter holiday meals. It holds a place of honor at Thanksgiving and Christmas tables, but is now appearing more regularly on year-round menus. Available in various sizes, turkey is perfect either for little meals or large get-togethers. It is excellent for buffets and, cooked on a spit, favored for outdoor dining.

Of our domesticated fowl, the old-favorite duckling and the newer Rock Cornish hen, are a pleasure to serve because they have the virtue of being unusual. Both are generally roasted, broiled or grilled outdoors. Many excellent stuffings and sauces may be served with them, and they blend well with fruit and sweet-sour flavorings.

❋ Bombay Chicken

2 pounds chicken parts
2 tablespoons shortening
1 can (10¾ ounces) condensed
  tomato soup
⅓ cup water
¼ cup chopped onion

1 medium clove garlic, minced
1 teaspoon curry powder
¼ teaspoon thyme, crushed
Toasted slivered almonds,
  flaked coconut, chutney,
  sliced green onions, and raisins

In skillet, brown chicken in shortening; pour off fat. Add soup, water, onion, garlic, curry, and thyme. Cover; cook over low heat 45 minutes or until chicken is tender. Stir now and then. Serve with a variety of the remaining ingredients. 4 servings.

❋ Chicken Marengo

3 pounds chicken parts
3 tablespoons shortening
1 can (10½ ounces) condensed
  golden mushroom soup

1 can (10¾ ounces) condensed
  tomato soup
1 medium clove garlic, minced
1 pound (about 16) small whole
  white onions

In large skillet, brown chicken in shortening; pour off fat. Stir in remaining ingredients. Cover; cook over low heat 45 minutes or until tender. Stir now and then. Uncover; cook until desired consistency. 6 servings.

Chicken Basque

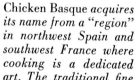
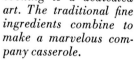

Chicken Basque *acquires its name from a "region" in northwest Spain and southwest France where cooking is a dedicated art. The traditional fine ingredients combine to make a marvelous company casserole.*

3 pounds chicken parts
2 tablespoons shortening
Salt and pepper
2 cans (10¾ ounces each)
  condensed tomato soup
¼ cup Chablis or other dry
  white wine

4 cups eggplant strips, ¾ inch
  thick (1 large eggplant)
½ pound mushrooms, quartered
½ cup diced cooked ham
½ cup chopped green pepper
2 medium cloves garlic, minced
⅛ teaspoon pepper
1 medium bay leaf

In large skillet, brown chicken in shortening. Transfer to 3-quart casserole; sprinkle with salt and pepper. Pour off fat in skillet; stir in soup and wine. Mix in remaining ingredients; pour over chicken. Cover; bake at 350° F. for 1 hour. 6 servings.

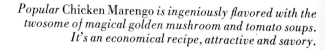

Popular Chicken Marengo *is ingeniously flavored with the twosome of magical golden mushroom and tomato soups. It's an economical recipe, attractive and savory.*

❋ Glorified Chicken

2 pounds chicken parts
2 tablespoons shortening

1 can (10¾ ounces) condensed
Cheddar cheese, cream of celery,
chicken, or mushroom soup

In skillet, brown chicken in shortening. Pour off fat. Stir in soup. Cover; cook over low heat 45 minutes or until tender. Stir now and then. 4 servings.

Oven Method: In shallow baking dish (12x8x2 inches), arrange chicken skin-side down. Pour 2 tablespoons butter over. Bake at 400°F. for 20 minutes. Turn chicken; bake 20 minutes more. Stir soup; pour over chicken. Bake 20 minutes more or until tender. Stir sauce before serving.

❋ Chicken Crunch

1 can (10½ ounces) condensed
cream of chicken, mushroom,
or golden mushroom soup*
¾ cup milk
1 tablespoon finely chopped
onion

1 tablespoon chopped parsley
2 pounds chicken parts
1 cup finely crushed packaged
herb seasoned stuffing mix
2 tablespoons melted butter or
margarine

Mix ⅓ cup soup, ¼ cup milk, onion, and parsley. Dip chicken in soup mixture; then roll in stuffing. Place in shallow baking dish (12x8x2 inches). Drizzle butter on chicken. Bake at 400°F. for 1 hour or until tender. Meanwhile, combine remaining soup and milk. Heat; stir now and then. Serve over chicken. 4 servings.

*When using golden mushroom soup, substitute water for milk.

Wine imparts a desirable subtle flavor to a dish and during the cooking the alcohol evaporates. The better the wine the better the dish. Use sparingly. Add after the poultry or meat has been browned.

❋ Coq au Vin

2 pounds chicken parts
2 tablespoons shortening
1 can (10½ ounces) condensed
chicken broth
1 can (4 ounces) mushroom
buttons, drained
⅓ cup Burgundy or other dry
red wine

10 small whole white onions
(about 8 ounces)
1 bay leaf
1 large clove garlic, minced
¼ teaspoon thyme, crushed
½ cup water
¼ cup flour

In skillet, brown chicken in shortening; pour off fat. Add broth, mushrooms, wine, onions, bay, garlic, and thyme. Cover; cook over low heat 45 minutes or until chicken and onions are tender. Stir now and then. Remove bay leaf. Gradually blend water into flour until smooth; slowly stir into sauce. Cook, stirring until thickened. 4 servings.

❋ Tetrazzini

2 tablespoons chopped onion
1 tablespoon butter or margarine
1 can (10½ ounces) condensed
   cream of mushroom soup
½ cup water
½ cup shredded sharp Cheddar
   cheese

1 tablespoon Sherry, optional
1 cup diced cooked chicken, turkey, or ham
2 tablespoons chopped pimiento
1 tablespoon chopped parsley
2 cups cooked spaghetti

In saucepan, cook onion in butter until tender. Blend in soup, water, cheese, and Sherry. Heat until cheese melts; stir now and then. Add chicken, pimiento, parsley, and spaghetti; heat. 3 servings.

❋ Chicken Cacciatore

2 pounds chicken parts
2 tablespoons shortening
1 can (10¾ ounces) condensed
   tomato soup
½ cup chopped onion
¼ cup Chianti or other dry red wine

2 large cloves garlic, minced
½ teaspoon oregano, crushed
⅛ teaspoon salt
½ medium green pepper, cut
   into strips

In skillet, brown chicken in shortening; pour off fat. Add remaining ingredients except pepper. Cover; cook over low heat 30 minutes. Add pepper. Cook 15 minutes more or until chicken is tender. Stir now and then. 4 servings.

❋ Chicken Via Veneto

4 pounds chicken parts
¼ cup butter or margarine
1 cup ham strips, optional
2 cans (10¾ ounces each)
   condensed Cheddar cheese soup

½ cup chopped canned tomatoes
3 medium onions, quartered.
½ teaspoon basil, crushed

Use 1 large skillet or prepare in 2 skillets (about 10 inch) by dividing ingredients equally. Brown chicken in butter; remove. Brown ham. Stir in soup, tomatoes, onions, and basil; add chicken. Cover; cook over low heat 45 minutes or until tender. Stir now and then. 8 servings.

Pages 82-83: Three gifts from Italy: Via Veneto, Tetrazzini and Chicken Cacciatore are triumphant main dishes for entertaining. Offer with any of them, a green salad, bread sticks, cheese and fruit.

Overstuffed Chicken

2 cans (10½ ounces each) con-
    densed golden mushroom soup
⅔ cup water
1 package (8 ounces) herb
    seasoned stuffing mix
¼ cup melted butter or
    margarine

2 broilers (about 2½ pounds
    each), split
Paprika
⅓ cup chopped onion
Generous dash poultry seasoning
2 tablespoons butter or
    margarine

Combine soup with water. In roasting pan (15½x10½x2¼ inches), mix ⅔ cup soup mixture with stuffing mix and melted butter. Place broilers over stuffing; sprinkle with paprika. Cover; bake at 400°F. for 1 hour. Uncover, bake 30 minutes longer or until tender. Meanwhile, in saucepan, cook onion with seasoning in butter until tender. Stir in remaining soup mixture. Heat; stir now and then. Serve with chicken and stuffing. 4 servings.

❋ Cordon Bleu

Cordon Bleu, *using chicken, is an excellent adaptation of the German veal, ham and cheese dish which was awarded the famed French blue ribbon in the late 1700s.*

3 whole chicken breasts (about
    2½ pounds), split, skinned,
    and boned
3 slices (4 ounces) Swiss cheese,
    cut in half
3 slices (4 ounces) boiled ham,
    cut in half

2 tablespoons butter or
    margarine
1 can (10½ ounces) condensed
    cream of chicken soup
¼ cup milk or light cream
Chopped parsley

Flatten chicken breasts with flat side of knife. Top each with ½ slice cheese, then ham; secure with toothpicks. In skillet, brown chicken-side down in butter. Stir in soup and milk. Cover; cook over low heat for 20 minutes or until tender. Stir now and then. Garnish with parsley. 6 servings.

Chicken Stephanie

2 chicken breasts (about 1½
    pounds), split
2 tablespoons shortening
1 can (10½ ounces) condensed
    cream of chicken soup

¼ cup light cream
¼ cup Sherry
1 package (6 ounces) frozen crab,
    thawed and drained

In skillet, brown chicken in shortening; pour off fat. Add remaining ingredients except crab. Cover; cook over low heat 30 minutes or until chicken is tender. Stir now and then. Add crab; heat. 4 servings.

Swedish Chicken Balls

1½ cups finely chopped cooked
    chicken or turkey
1 can (10½ ounces) condensed
    cream of celery soup
½ cup bread crumbs
2 eggs, slightly beaten

¼ teaspoon marjoram, crushed
¼ teaspoon salt
Generous dash pepper
2 tablespoons butter or margarine
¾ cup milk
¼ teaspoon chervil, crushed

Combine chicken, ¼ cup soup, crumbs, eggs, marjoram, salt, and pepper; mix
well. Shape into 16 balls. In skillet, brown balls in butter. Stir in remaining
soup, milk, and chervil. Cover; cook over low heat 10 minutes. Stir now and
then. 4 servings.

Arroz con Pollo

2 pounds chicken parts
2 tablespoons salad oil
1 can (10½ ounces) condensed
    chicken broth
1 can (1 pound) tomatoes, cut-up
⅓ cup water
½ cup chopped onion
2 medium cloves garlic, minced
1 teaspoon salt

¼ teaspoon saffron, crushed, or
    turmeric
⅛ teaspoon pepper
1 bay leaf
1 package (10 ounces) frozen
    peas
1 cup raw regular rice
¼ cup sliced stuffed or ripe
    olives

In skillet, brown chicken in oil; pour off fat. Add broth, tomatoes, water, onion,
garlic, salt, saffron, pepper, and bay. Cover; cook over low heat 15 minutes. Add
remaining ingredients. Cover; cook 30 minutes more or until chicken and rice are
tender; stir now and then. 4 servings.

❋ Quick Chicken Divan

1 package (10 ounces) frozen
    asparagus or broccoli spears,
    cooked and drained
3 to 4 servings sliced cooked
    chicken or turkey

1 can (10½ ounces) condensed
    cream of chicken or
    mushroom soup
⅓ cup milk
½ cup shredded Cheddar cheese

Layer asparagus in a shallow baking dish (10x6x2 inches); top with sliced chicken.
Blend soup and milk; pour over all; sprinkle with cheese. Broil about 4 to 5 inches
from heat until hot and lightly browned on top—about 8 minutes. (Or bake at
450°F.—about 15 minutes.) 3 to 4 servings.

Baked Fondue

4 eggs, separated
1 can (10½ ounces) condensed
   cream of mushroom soup
2 cups dry bread cubes
1 cup diced cooked chicken or turkey
⅓ cup shredded sharp process cheese

¼ cup toasted slivered almonds
1 tablespoon grated onion
1 tablespoon chopped parsley
⅛ teaspoon marjoram, crushed
⅛ teaspoon thyme, crushed

Beat egg whites until stiff but not dry; beat yolks until thick. Combine yolks, soup, bread, chicken, cheese, almonds, onion, and herbs; gently fold in whites. Pour into 1½-quart casserole. Bake at 325°F. for 1 hour. 4 servings.

❋ 3-Way a la King

2 tablespoons chopped green pepper
¼ cup chopped onion
2 tablespoons butter or margarine
1 can (10½ ounces) condensed cream
   of chicken or mushroom soup

⅓ to ½ cup milk
1 to 1½ cups cubed cooked
   chicken, ham, or turkey
2 tablespoons diced pimiento
Patty shells, toast, or rice

In saucepan, cook green pepper and onion in butter until tender. Blend in soup and milk; add chicken and pimiento. Heat; stir now and then. Serve in patty shells. 3 to 4 servings.

Chicken Kiev

½ cup butter or margarine, softened
1 tablespoon chopped parsley
1 medium clove garlic, minced
¼ teaspoon rosemary, crushed
Dash pepper
3 chicken breasts (about 2½
   pounds), split, skinned, and boned
1 egg, slightly beaten

½ cup fine dry bread crumbs
2 tablespoons chopped onion
1 tablespoon chopped parsley
2 tablespoons butter or margarine
1 can (10½ ounces) condensed
   cream of chicken soup
⅓ cup milk
2 tablespoons Sherry or brandy

Blend together ½ cup butter, parsley, garlic, rosemary, and pepper. On waxed paper, form patty ¾-inch thick; place in freezer until firm. Meanwhile, flatten chicken breasts with meat hammer or edge of heavy saucer to ¼-inch thickness. Cut butter into 6 equal pieces; place one in center of each breast. Tuck in ends and roll tightly. Secure with toothpicks or skewers. Dip in egg and then in bread crumbs. Chill. In saucepan, cook onion with parsley in 2 tablespoons butter until tender. Blend in soup, milk, and Sherry. Heat; stir now and then. Fry 2 breast rolls at a time in deep fat at 350°F. for 10 to 12 minutes until well browned. Drain on absorbent paper. Serve with sauce. 6 servings.

Brunswick Stew

2 slices bacon
2 pounds chicken parts
½ cup sliced onion
1 medium clove garlic, minced
1 can (10¾ ounces) condensed
tomato soup
⅓ cup water

1 teaspoon Worcestershire
¼ teaspoon salt
Dash pepper
1 package (10 ounces) frozen
okra
1 package (10 ounces) frozen
succotash

The place of origin of Brunswick Stew, a favorite southern dish, is disputed. It is claimed by Brunswick County, Georgia; Brunswick County, Virginia; and Brunswick County, North Carolina.

In large pan, cook bacon until crisp; remove and crumble. Pour off all but 2 tablespoons drippings. Brown chicken and cook onion with garlic in drippings until tender. Stir in soup, water, Worcestershire, salt, and pepper. Cover; cook over low heat 15 minutes. Add vegetables. Cook 30 minutes more or until tender, stirring vegetables into sauce. Garnish with bacon. 4 servings.

Old Fashioned Chicken and Noodles

1 can (10½ ounces) condensed
cream of chicken soup
⅓ cup milk
1½ cups diced cooked chicken
1½ cups cooked noodles
1 cup cooked corn

¼ cup finely chopped onion
¼ teaspoon paprika or saffron,
crushed
Generous dash pepper
¼ cup buttered bread crumbs
1 hard-cooked egg, sliced

In 1½-quart casserole, blend soup and milk; stir in chicken, noodles, corn, onion, paprika, and pepper. Top with crumbs. Bake at 350° F. for 30 minutes or until hot. Garnish with egg. 4 servings.

Chicken Asparagus Pie

1 can (10½ ounces) condensed
cream of celery soup
1 cup cubed cooked chicken
2 hard-cooked eggs, coarsely
chopped
1 package (10 ounces) frozen cut
asparagus, cooked and drained

⅓ cup finely chopped celery
2 tablespoons chopped pimiento
⅓ cup Sherry
Dash mace
9-inch pie crust

In 9-inch round shallow baking dish, combine all ingredients except pastry. Cover with pastry; make several slits on top. Bake at 450° F. for 20 minutes or until done. 4 servings.

Livers Paprikash

1 package (8 ounces) frozen
 chicken livers, thawed
1/2 cup chopped celery
1/2 cup chopped onion
2 tablespoons butter or margarine

1 can (10 1/2 ounces) condensed
 cream of chicken or mushroom
 soup
1/3 cup milk
1/2 teaspoon paprika
Toast

In saucepan, brown chicken livers and cook celery and onion in butter until tender. Stir in soup, milk, and paprika. Heat; stir now and then. Serve over toast. 4 servings.

Hot Club Sandwich

4 servings sliced cooked chicken
8 slices cooked bacon
4 tomato slices
4 slices toast

1 can (10 3/4 ounces) condensed
 Cheddar cheese soup
1/2 cup sour cream

Arrange chicken, bacon, and tomato on each slice of toast. In saucepan, blend soup and sour cream. Heat; stir now and then. Pour over sandwiches. Makes 4 open-face sandwiches.

Duckling Montmorency

1 duckling (about 5 pounds)
1/2 teaspoon salt
1/8 teaspoon pepper
Dash ground thyme
1 can (16 ounces) pitted dark
 sweet cherries

1/2 to 3/4 cup Port or other sweet
 red wine
1 can (10 1/2 ounces) condensed
 beef broth
1 tablespoon lemon juice
1 tablespoon cornstarch

Season cavity of duckling with salt, pepper, and thyme. Prick skin and place breast-side up on rack in shallow baking pan. Roast at 325° F. for about 3 hours (30 to 35 minutes per pound or until tender). Meanwhile, drain cherries, reserving 1/4 cup of the liquid. Let cherries stand in Port. Drain juices from cavity and remove duckling to serving platter; keep warm. Skim fat from drippings; add Port drained from cherries. Bring to boil; stir to loosen browned bits. Add broth, cherries, and lemon juice. Blend cornstarch into reserved cherry liquid; add to roasting pan. Cook, stirring constantly until thickened and clear. Spoon some sauce over duckling; serve remaining. 4 servings.

Regal fare that features a wine-flavored cherry sauce: Duckling Montmorency.

CHEESE EGGS · PASTA

These three favorite foods have an affinity for each other and combine harmoniously in delightful culinary creations. They also have great appeal when cooked separately or with other enticing fare.

We relish cheese, by itself, as snack, appetizer and dessert. Very popular, too, are soups, sauces, souffles, casseroles and pasta creations made with cheeses. In recent years Switzerland's fondue has proved an intriguing addition to the list.

A good selection of cheeses, both domestic and imported, is now available. Fortunately, many of them are interchangeable in recipes. We have become well acquainted with the qualities and uses of the basic types, such as cottage or Cheddar, as well as more exotic ones like ricotta, Muenster, and Camembert.

If any food is all-important to cookery, it must be the egg. By itself, it is nutritious and appealing. And it is significant in many other roles in cookery—thickening sauces, binding ingredients, garnishing foods. Eggs are served for every meal and have a place in every course. Poached, fried, baked, scrambled, hard-cooked or made into omelets, they combine with other foods to make attractive party dishes. Eggs are elementary, economical but also exceptional and elegant.

The preparation of pasta has become extremely popular in America in recent years. Fortunately a galaxy of fascinating pasta products—lasagna, manicotti, spaghetti, macaroni and vermicelli—is readily available in our stores. Pasta dishes are valued for entertaining as they can be prepared ahead of time and are most attractive served in casseroles for buffets or informal dining.

Saucy Baked Eggs

1 can (10½ ounces) condensed
  cream of chicken soup
⅓ cup light cream
½ cup shredded natural Swiss
  cheese

2 tablespoons grated Parmesan
  cheese
10 eggs

In saucepan, combine all ingredients except eggs. Heat until cheese melts; stir now and then. For each serving, break two eggs into individual baking dishes or custard cups (6-ounce size); cover with sauce. Sprinkle with additional Parmesan cheese. Bake at 350°F. for 10 to 15 minutes until eggs are desired doneness. 5 servings.

Huevos Rancheros

¼ cup chopped onion
2 to 3 teaspoons chili powder
1 large clove garlic, minced
2 tablespoons butter or
  margarine

1 can (10¾ ounces) condensed
  tomato soup
½ cup water
6 eggs
6 slices toast or tortillas

In skillet, cook onion with chili and garlic in butter until tender. Add soup and water; bring to boil. Gently slip eggs into soup sauce. Cover; cook over low heat until whites are firm. Serve eggs on toast with sauce. 6 servings.

❋ Easy Souffle

1 can (10½ ounces) condensed
  cream of celery, chicken, or
  mushroom soup
1 cup shredded sharp process
  cheese

2 to 3 teaspoons curry powder,
  optional
6 eggs, separated

In saucepan, combine soup and cheese; add curry powder, if desired. Heat slowly until cheese melts. Stir now and then. Remove from heat. Beat egg yolks until thick and lemon colored; gradually stir in soup mixture. In large bowl, beat egg whites until stiff; fold soup mixture into egg whites. Pour into ungreased 2-quart casserole. Bake at 300°F. about 1 to 1¼ hours or until souffle is brown. Serve immediately. 4 to 6 servings.

Puffy Omelet with Avocado Sauce

Omelet:

6 eggs, separated
1/3 cup milk
1/4 teaspoon salt

Dash pepper
3 tablespoons butter
    or margarine

Beat egg whites until stiff. Beat yolks until thick and lemon colored; beat in milk, salt, pepper; fold into whites. Heat butter in oven-proof skillet; pour in eggs. Cook over low heat about 5 minutes or until lightly browned on bottom. Bake at 350°F. for 10 to 15 minutes or until top springs back when pressed with finger.

Sauce:

1/4 cup sliced green onions
1 teaspoon curry powder
1 tablespoon butter or margarine
1 can (10½ ounces) condensed
    cream of mushroom soup

1/3 cup milk
1 teaspoon lemon juice
1 small avocado, peeled and
    cubed

Meanwhile, in saucepan, cook onions with curry in butter until tender. Add soup, milk, and lemon juice. Heat; stir now and then. Add avocado just before serving. When omelet is done, transfer to platter. Make a shallow cut down the center; pour part of sauce on; fold in half. Top with remaining sauce. 4 servings.

❊ Crispy Macaroni and Cheese

1 can (10½ ounces) condensed
    cream of celery or mushroom soup
1/2 cup milk
1/2 teaspoon prepared mustard

Generous dash pepper
3 cups cooked elbow macaroni
2 cups shredded Cheddar cheese
1 cup French fried onions

In 1½-quart casserole, blend soup, milk, mustard, and pepper. Stir in macaroni and 1½ cups cheese. Bake at 350°F. for 20 minutes. Top with onions and remaining cheese; bake 10 minutes more. 4 servings.

❊ Spaghetti with White Clam Sauce

1 can (7½ ounces) minced clams
2 medium cloves garlic, minced
2 tablespoons chopped parsley
2 tablespoons butter or margarine
1 can (10½ ounces) condensed
    cream of mushroom soup

1/4 cup milk or light cream
1 to 2 tablespoons grated
    Parmesan cheese
1/2 pound spaghetti, cooked and
    drained

Drain clams; reserve liquid. In saucepan, cook clams, garlic, and parsley in butter a few minutes. Stir in soup, milk, clam liquid, and cheese. Cook over low heat 10 minutes. Stir now and then. Serve over spaghetti. 2 servings.

❋ Spaghetti with Meat Sauce

1 pound ground beef
1 cup chopped onion
1 teaspoon basil, crushed
2 teaspoons oregano, crushed
2 large cloves garlic, minced

2 cans (10¾ ounces each)
  condensed tomato soup
1 can (1 pound) tomatoes
½ pound spaghetti, cooked and
  drained
Grated Parmesan cheese

In saucepan, brown beef and cook onion with seasonings until onion is tender. Add soup and tomatoes. Stir to break up tomatoes. Cook over low heat 45 minutes; stir now and then. Serve over spaghetti with Parmesan. 4 servings.

❋ Lasagna

½ pound ground beef
1 cup chopped onion
2 large cloves garlic, minced
2 teaspoons oregano, crushed
2 cans (10¾ ounces each)
  condensed tomato soup
½ cup water
2 teaspoons vinegar

9 lasagna noodles (about
  ½ pound), cooked and
  drained
1 pint cream-style cottage
  cheese or ricotta cheese
5 slices (½ pound)
  Mozzarella cheese
Grated Parmesan cheese

Available to today's cook are over 100 pasta products. Get to know a variety of them to make memorable and rewarding fare.

In saucepan, brown beef and cook onion, garlic, and oregano until onion is tender. Add soup, water, and vinegar. Cook over low heat 30 minutes; stir now and then. In shallow baking dish (12x8x2 inches), arrange 3 alternate layers of noodles, cottage cheese, meat sauce, and Mozzarella cheese. Sprinkle with Parmesan cheese. Bake at 350°F. for 30 minutes. Let stand 15 minutes before serving. 6 servings.

❋ Fettuccini

1 can (10½ ounces) condensed
  cream of mushroom or
  tomato soup*
¾ cup milk

½ cup grated Parmesan cheese
3 cups hot cooked noodles
4 tablespoons butter
  or margarine

In large saucepan, stir soup until smooth; blend in milk and cheese. Heat; stir now and then. *Just before serving,* toss *hot* noodles with butter; combine with soup mixture. Serve with additional cheese. 4 servings.

*When using tomato soup substitute light cream for milk.

Bring a little of the magic of Rome to your table with any one of these pasta specialties: Fettuccini, Spaghetti *and* Lasagna.

VEGETABLES

Seek variety when you select and cook vegetables. Despite the diverse types of these delicious and colorful foods, we too often offer the same familiar vegetables prepared in the simplest manner. We tend to take them for granted and fail to treat them with imagination.

The art of vegetable cookery is one of the easiest to master. Vegetables, whether frozen, canned or fresh, should be cooked until just tender. For a change from the usual, serve braised, baked or stuffed vegetables to enhance a meal. Prepare them also as souffles, or cooked with piquant sauces. They may become a specialty of the house. Herbs and seasonings give new dimensions even to ordinary carrots, spinach or peas.

Over the centuries the social status of vegetables has changed and fluctuated remarkably. Mushrooms were not really accepted here as a culinary marvel until recent years. The potato was shunned in both the Old and New World, from whence it came, until its beneficial qualities as a food were finally realized, only in the early 1700s. Two "relatives," the eggplant and tomato, dubbed the "mad apple" and "love apple," were long suspected to be poisonous and even in colonial America were grown as curiosities.

All vegetables are worthy of interest. Attractive to serve, they may be delectable appetizers, first courses, side dishes or main dishes for luncheons and suppers. Remember too, that they add particular sparkle and color to a buffet or dinner table.

In vegetable cookery there is great opportunity for imaginative preparation and serving to lift these foods out of the background and make them a special attraction both for everyday and company meals.

Stuffed Zucchini

6 small zucchini (about 2 pounds)
½ pound ground beef
⅓ cup chopped onion
1 large clove garlic, minced
1 teaspoon oregano, crushed

2 tablespoons olive oil
1 can (11 ounces) condensed
  bisque of tomato soup
¼ cup grated Parmesan cheese

Cut lengthwise slice from top of zucchini; scoop out seeds and pulp leaving ¼-inch shell. Coarsely chop pulp and seeds. In skillet, brown beef and cook onion, garlic, and oregano in oil until onion is tender. Add zucchini pulp and seeds, ¼ cup soup, and Parmesan. Spoon into zucchini shells; arrange in shallow baking dish (12x8x2 inches). Pour remaining soup over and around stuffed zucchini; sprinkle with additional Parmesan. Cover; bake at 375°F. for 40 minutes or until tender. Uncover; bake 5 minutes more. 6 servings.

The carrot, a very ancient vegetable, rates today as a staple in almost every kitchen. Eaten both in its delightfully crisp raw state as well as cooked, it also wins praise for its rich hue (orange is sometimes described as the most "edible" color).

Holiday Carrots and Onions

1 pound (about 8) carrots,
  halved lengthwise
1 pound (about 18) small
  whole white onions

1 can (10½ ounces) condensed
  cream of mushroom soup
1 tablespoon chopped parsley
¼ teaspoon paprika
Toasted slivered almonds

Cut carrots in 3-inch pieces. In covered saucepan, cook carrots and onions in water for 30 minutes or until tender. Drain. Stir in soup, ½ cup water, parsley, and paprika. Heat; stir now and then. Garnish with almonds. 6 to 8 servings.

Honey Glazed Sweet Potatoes

1 can (10½ ounces) condensed
  consomme
¼ cup honey
1 tablespoon cornstarch
1 teaspoon grated orange rind

Generous dash cinnamon
4 medium sweet potatoes
  (about 2 pounds), cooked,
  peeled, and cut in half

In skillet, combine all ingredients except potatoes. Cook, stirring until thickened. Add potatoes. Cook over low heat 10 minutes or until potatoes are glazed, basting frequently. 4 to 6 servings.

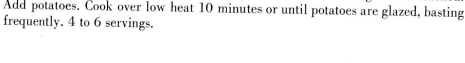

Capture the accolades of your guests by surprising them with different vegetable creations. This trio: Stuffed Zucchini, Holiday Carrots and Onions *and* Honey Glazed Sweet Potatoes.

❋ Easy Creamed Vegetables

*2 packages (9 to 10 ounces each) frozen cauliflower, corn, green beans, lima
beans, mixed vegetables, peas, peas and carrots, carrots, or spinach*
1 can (10½ ounces) condensed cream of celery, chicken, or mushroom soup

Cook vegetables in unsalted water until tender; drain. Stir in soup. Heat; stir now
and then. Thin to desired consistency with milk. 6 servings.

❋ Green Bean Bake

*1 can (10½ ounces) condensed
    cream of mushroom soup*
⅓ cup milk
1 teaspoon soy sauce
Dash pepper

*2 packages (9 ounces each)
    frozen green beans, cooked
    and drained*
*1 can (3½ ounces) French
    fried onions*

In 1-quart casserole, stir soup, milk, soy, and pepper until smooth; mix in green
beans and ½ can onions. Bake at 350°F. for 25 minutes; stir. Top with remaining onions. Bake 5 minutes more. 6 servings.

Ratatouille

3 small zucchini, sliced (3 cups)
*2 medium green peppers, cut
    into strips*
1 cup sliced onion
1 large clove garlic, minced
½ teaspoon basil, crushed

2 tablespoons olive oil
*1 can (10¾ ounces)
    condensed tomato soup*
*1 medium eggplant, peeled and
    cubed*
½ teaspoon salt

In skillet, cook zucchini, green pepper, onion, garlic, and basil in oil 5 minutes.
Add remaining ingredients. Cover; cook over low heat 25 minutes. Stir now and
then. Uncover; cook 5 minutes more. 8 to 10 servings.

Potato Pancakes

*1 can (10½ ounces) condensed
    cream of potato soup*
⅓ cup flour
3 eggs

2 tablespoons bacon drippings
½ cup canned corn
*2 slices bacon, cooked and
    crumbled*
Applesauce or maple syrup

In bowl, blend soup and flour; beat in eggs and drippings. Add corn and bacon.
Pour ¼ cup batter for each pancake on hot, lightly greased griddle. Cook until
golden brown on each side; turn only once. Serve with applesauce or syrup.
Makes 10 pancakes.

Stuffed Acorn Squash

3 acorn squash
Butter
Salt and pepper
¾ pound ground beef
¼ pound bulk sausage

½ cup chopped celery
⅓ cup chopped onion
1 can (10½ ounces) condensed
  cream of mushroom soup
Buttered bread crumbs

Split squash; remove seeds and fibers. Brush inside and edge with butter; sprinkle with salt and pepper. Bake cut side down in shallow baking dish at 400°F. for 35 minutes. Meanwhile, in skillet, cook beef, sausage, celery, and onion until meat is browned and celery is tender. Stir in soup. Fill squash with mixture; top with crumbs. Bake 20 minutes more or until tender. 6 servings.

Chinese Vegetables

2 cups diagonally sliced celery
1 cup diagonally sliced green
  onion
2 tablespoons salad oil
1 can (10½ ounces) condensed
  chicken broth
1 can (5 ounces) bamboo
  shoots, drained

1 can (1 pound) bean sprouts,
  drained
1 can (5 ounces) water
  chestnuts, drained and
  sliced
2 tablespoons cornstarch
2 tablespoons soy sauce
Cooked rice

The Chinese regard vegetables with high esteem and have perfected the art of cooking them. By using their quick-fry method, vegetables remain crisp, keep their original color and retain valuable nutrients.

In skillet, cook celery and onion in oil until just tender. Add remaining ingredients except rice. Cook over low heat, stirring until thickened. Serve over rice. Serve with additional soy sauce. 6 servings.

Onions with Sausage Stuffing

4 large onions (about 2 pounds),
  peeled
¼ pound bulk sausage
½ teaspoon herb seasoning
1 can (10½ ounces) condensed
  cream of mushroom soup

¼ cup bread crumbs
½ cup milk
⅛ teaspoon marjoram,
  crushed

In saucepan, cook onions in boiling water 15 minutes; drain. Cut tops off onions; scoop out centers leaving ¼-inch thick shell. Chop onion centers. In skillet, cook sausage with chopped onion and herb seasoning until done; mix in ¼ cup soup and crumbs. Firmly fill onion shells with sausage mixture; arrange in 9-inch pie dish. Add water to just cover bottom of dish. Bake at 350°F. for 40 minutes. Meanwhile in saucepan, combine remaining soup, milk, and marjoram; heat. Serve over onions. 4 servings.

Vegetables a la Grecque

Despite the name this colorful vegetable medley is a most popular hors d'oeuvre in lovely French Provence along the Mediterranean. It is also a marvelous accompaniment to meat, poultry or game.

Vegetables:

2 cups water
9 small whole white onions
   (½ pound)
2 cups whole green beans
   (¼ pound)
2½ cups cauliflowerets
   (½ pound)
2 cups celery strips (¼ pound)
1 package (9 ounces) frozen
   artichokes
2 cups small fresh mushroom
   caps (about ¼ pound)

Marinade:

1 can (10½ ounces)
   condensed chicken broth
½ soup can water
⅓ cup lemon juice
¼ cup olive oil
3 large cloves garlic, minced
2 large bay leaves
1 teaspoon fennel seed
12 peppercorns
½ teaspoon ground coriander
½ teaspoon ground thyme

In large saucepan, bring water to boil; add onions and beans. Cover; cook over low heat 10 minutes. Add cauliflower and celery; cook 5 minutes more. Add artichokes; cook 5 minutes more. Add mushrooms; cook 5 minutes or until vegetables are just tender; drain. Combine ingredients for marinade; add to vegetables. Cover; bring to boil. Chill; stir now and then. Arrange drained vegetables on platter; moisten with a few spoonfuls of marinade. Makes 6 cups vegetables.

Baked Stuffed Tomatoes

6 medium tomatoes
2 slices bacon
¼ cup chopped green pepper
¼ cup chopped onion
1 cup cooked corn
Generous dash pepper

¾ cup toasted buttered bread
   cubes
1 can (10½ ounces) condensed
   cream of celery soup
¼ cup milk

Cut slice from top of tomatoes; scoop out and save pulp leaving ¼-inch shell. In skillet, cook bacon; remove and crumble. Cook green pepper and onion in drippings until tender; stir in corn, pepper, and all but ½ cup tomato pulp. Cook over low heat 5 minutes. Place 1 tablespoon bread in each tomato; fill with vegetable mixture. Top with remaining bread. Place in baking dish; add water to just cover bottom of dish. Bake at 350°F. for 20 minutes. Meanwhile in saucepan, combine soup, reserved tomato pulp, milk, and bacon; heat but do not boil. Serve over tomatoes. 6 servings.

❄ *Broccoli au Gratin*

1 bunch broccoli (about 2
  pounds) or 1 small head
  cauliflower (or two 10-ounce
  frozen packages of either
  vegetable)
1 can (10¾ ounces) condensed
  Cheddar cheese soup

¼ cup milk
2 tablespoons buttered bread
  crumbs
4 slices bacon, cooked and
  crumbled

Cook vegetable; drain. Place in shallow baking dish (10 x 6 x 2 inches). Stir soup; blend in milk; pour over vegetable. Top with crumbs. Bake at 350°F. for 20 minutes or until hot. Garnish with bacon before serving. 4 to 6 servings.

Minted Creamed Peas and Celery

2 cups thinly sliced celery
¼ teaspoon salt
1 cup water
1 package (10 ounces) frozen
  peas

1 can (10½ ounces) condensed
  cream of chicken soup
⅓ cup milk
1 teaspoon lemon juice
¼ teaspoon dried mint flakes,
  crushed

In saucepan, combine celery, salt, and water. Cook for 15 minutes or until just tender. Add peas; bring to boil. Cover; cook over low heat 5 minutes or until tender. Drain; add remaining ingredients. Heat; stir now and then. 4 to 6 servings.

Sweet Sour Cabbage

2 slices bacon
½ cup chopped onion
1 can (10½ ounces) condensed
  chicken broth
⅓ cup wine vinegar
2 tablespoons sugar
Generous dash pepper

3 cups thinly sliced tart
  apples (2 medium)
1 medium bay leaf
7 cups shredded red cabbage,
  1 small head (about 1½
  pounds)
1 tablespoon cornstarch
2 tablespoons water

In northern and central Europe this is one of the most prized vegetable dishes. It is excellent with pork, game or goose, and is a traditional Christmas dish in many countries.

In skillet, cook bacon; remove and crumble. Cook onion in drippings until tender. Stir in broth, vinegar, sugar, pepper; add apple and bay. Bring to boil; add cabbage. Cover; cook over medium heat 45 minutes or until tender. Combine cornstarch and water; stir into cabbage. Cook, stirring until slightly thickened. Garnish with bacon. 6 servings.

SALADS and DRESSINGS

"**A** fool can pick a sallet as well as a wise man," goes an old saying. But which salad to choose is another matter, since tastes in salads differ so widely. Fortunately, the variety available permits a selection agreeable to everyone.

In ancient days salads were simply made with edible greens or herbs over which oil, vinegar and spices were poured. The word salad comes from the Latin "sal" or salt, which the Romans commonly used as a food preservative. In Europe salads did not really become fashionable or popular until the 1700s when court cooks, who set the culinary styles, combined numerous ingredients to make them. The vogue in England was to include several kinds of flower petals. "They say primroses make a capital salad," wrote Disraeli.

Today we Americans have become enamored of salads and they now appear in infinite variety. Although generally served cold, some are offered hot. They may be appetizers, first courses, main or side dishes.

World-wide tastes for salads vary greatly. In the Orient they are customarily pickled foods. The French serve salads as appetizers or as a separate course after the entree. A favorite in Germany is made with sauerkraut. In the Middle East they are most often fresh vegetables flavored with oil and lemon juice. South of the border many salads are based on avocados. A salad cart with a display of many varieties in European restaurants is a delight to behold.

In America we have embraced salads from around the world and contributed molded salads made with gelatine, as well as those utilizing fruit, cheeses, and sometimes nuts and raisins. Very important to salads are the many dressings, which can be purchased or homemade.

Chef's Salad with Blue Cheese-Mushroom Dressing

1 medium head lettuce, torn in
    pieces
1 package (10 ounces) frozen
    asparagus spears, cooked,
    drained, and chilled
1 cup cooked chicken cut in strips
1 cup cooked ham cut in strips
2 hard-cooked eggs, sliced

1 can (10½ ounces) condensed
    cream of mushroom or
    celery soup
½ cup sour cream
¼ cup crumbled blue cheese
2 tablespoons milk
1 tablespoon lemon juice

Place lettuce in salad bowl. Top with an arrangement of asparagus, chicken, ham, and eggs. For dressing, combine remaining ingredients and stir until smooth. Thin to desired consistency with additional milk. Chill. Serve with salad. 4 servings.

Serve sparkling salad...either Ribbon Aspic or Chef's as the main course for a special luncheon.

Ribbon Aspic

Cheese Layer:

1 envelope unflavored gelatine
½ cup milk
3 cups cottage cheese
½ cup chopped cucumber
2 tablespoons minced onion

Aspic Layer:

1 envelope unflavored gelatine
½ cup cold water
1 can (10¾ ounces) condensed
    tomato soup
1 tablespoon lemon juice
½ teaspoon dried dill leaves, crushed
1½ cups diced cooked shrimp

In saucepan, sprinkle 1 envelope gelatine on milk to soften. Place over low heat, stirring until gelatine is dissolved. Remove from heat; stir in cheese, cucumber, and onion. In bottom of loaf pan (9x5x3 inches), spoon in half of cheese mixture. Chill until slightly firm. Meanwhile, in saucepan, sprinkle 1 envelope gelatine on ½ cup cold water to soften. Place over low heat, stirring until gelatine is dissolved. Remove from heat; stir in soup, juice, and dill. Chill until slightly thickened. Fold in shrimp. Pour onto cheese layer. Chill until slightly firm. Top with remaining cheese mixture. Chill until firm. Unmold; garnish with shrimp, cucumber, and pimiento strips, if desired. 6 to 8 servings.

❋ Potato-Ham Salad

1 can (10½ ounces) condensed
    cream of celery soup
¼ cup water
2 teaspoons vinegar
⅛ teaspoon pepper
3 cups cubed cooked potatoes

1½ cups cubed cooked ham
¼ cup diced sweet pickle
2 tablespoons minced green
    onion
Sliced hard-cooked egg
Parsley sprigs

In large bowl, blend soup, water, vinegar, and pepper. Add potatoes, ham, pickle, and onion. Chill. Garnish with egg and parsley. 4 servings.

To serve hot: Increase water to ½ cup. In skillet, prepare as above. Heat; stir now and then.

Cucumbers in Sour Cream Dressing

1 can (10½ ounces) condensed
    cream of celery soup
½ cup sour cream
2 tablespoons finely chopped dill
    pickle
2 tablespoons finely chopped
    onion

2 tablespoons finely chopped
    radishes
Generous dash pepper
4 cups thinly sliced cucumber
    (about 4 medium cucumbers)
Lettuce
Parsley

Mix soup, sour cream, pickle, onion, radish, and pepper; add cucumbers. Chill. Serve on lettuce; garnish with parsley and additional radishes. 6 to 8 servings.

Remoulade Dressing

1 can (10½ ounces) condensed
    cream of celery soup
⅓ cup mayonnaise
¼ cup chopped sweet pickle
1 tablespoon capers, drained

1 tablespoon chopped anchovies
1 tablespoon chopped parsley
¼ teaspoon dry mustard
Generous dash crushed tarragon

Thoroughly mix all ingredients. Chill. Thin with additional milk if desired. Serve with cold sliced chicken or flaked crab meat on salad greens. Makes about 2 cups dressing.

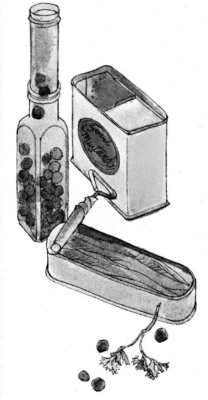

Molded Borsch

1 envelope unflavored gelatine
¾ cup cold water
1 can (10½ ounces) condensed
  consomme

1 can (8 ounces) diced beets
1 tablespoon lemon juice
2 tablespoons thinly sliced green
  onion
1 cup sour cream

In saucepan, sprinkle gelatine on cold water to soften. Place over low heat, stirring until gelatine is dissolved. Remove from heat; stir in consomme, liquid from beets, and lemon juice. Chill until slightly thickened. Fold in beets and 1 tablespoon onion. Pour into 4-cup ring mold and chill until firm. Unmold on lettuce. Fill center of mold with sour cream; garnish with remaining onion. 4 servings.

Molded Borsch *translates the beloved Polish and Russian soup into sparkling ruby salad. Bright to see and taste.*

Tomatoes with Shrimp Stuffing

1 can (10½ ounces) condensed
  cream of asparagus soup
½ cup sour cream
1 teaspoon lemon juice
¼ teaspoon Worcestershire
⅛ teaspoon dried dill leaves

2 cups diced cooked shrimp
½ cup diced cucumber
¼ cup chopped green pepper
4 medium tomatoes
Salad greens

In bowl, blend soup, sour cream, lemon juice, Worcestershire, and dill. Add shrimp, cucumber, and green pepper; chill. Place tomatoes stem end down. Cut down almost to stem but not quite through making 5 slices. Place on greens; fill between slices with shrimp mixture. 4 servings.

❈ Tomato French Dressing
Pictured on back cover

1 can (10¾ ounces) condensed
  tomato soup
½ cup salad oil

¼ cup vinegar
½ teaspoon dry mustard

Combine ingredients in a jar; shake well before using. (Or mix in an electric blender.) Makes about 1½ cups dressing. Serve with salad greens.

Variations: To 1 recipe of Tomato French Dressing add any one of the following:
  · 4 slices bacon, cooked and crumbled
  · ¼ cup crumbled blue cheese
  · 1 medium clove garlic, minced
  · ¼ cup sweet pickle relish

BARBECUES

One of the most popular forms of entertaining is the barbecue. It presents the hostess with an opportunity to create an informal and attractive occasion with a minimum of effort. Whether enjoyed indoors or out, much of the preparation can be done beforehand, and it is not unusual for the host to participate in the culinary chores.

It was probably in pre-historic times that man discovered, doubtlessly by accident, the miracles that fire worked upon his food. Later, roaming herdsmen found that tough mutton, cut into small pieces, marinated and cooked on sticks over low fires, tasted much better than before. Archaeological finds in the Middle East testify that as early as 3000 B.C. man was utilizing movable metal hearths, metal spits and other gadgetry to enhance preparation of his food.

In medieval Europe whole carcasses of animals were cooked on spits, often in the dining hall fireplace. Our colonial forefathers used large kitchen fireplaces or outside shelters for this type of cookery.

Over the decades American cooks have devised fascinating recipes for favorite meats, poultry and seafood in barbecue sauces. The popularity of outdoor cookery on grills, hibachis, or over open fires has reached new peaks. Many of the same or different dishes can be prepared in our excellent indoor ovens or electric rotisseries, and enjoyed in the dining room, or brought to the patio, porch or backyard.

We are all fond of these appealing foods in their savory combinations. Excellent for family get-togethers and entertaining friends, the barbecue lets everyone enjoy the tantalizing aromas of the actual cookery, and then the irresistible results.

❊ All 'Round Barbecue Sauce

*1 can (10¾ ounces) condensed
   tomato soup
2 to 4 tablespoons sweet pickle
   relish*

*¼ cup chopped onion
1 tablespoon brown sugar
1 tablespoon vinegar
1 tablespoon Worcestershire*

In saucepan, combine all ingredients. Cover; cook over low heat 10 minutes. Stir now and then. Makes 1½ cups sauce.

❊ Zippy Barbecue Sauce

*⅓ cup chopped onion
1 small clove garlic, minced
2 tablespoons salad oil
1 can (10¾ ounces) condensed
   tomato soup*

*2 tablespoons brown sugar
1 tablespoon vinegar
1 to 2 tablespoons Worcestershire
1 teaspoon prepared mustard
Dash hot pepper sauce*

In saucepan, cook onion and garlic in oil until tender; add remaining ingredients. Cook over low heat 15 minutes; stir now and then. Makes 1½ cups sauce.

Note: Use either of the above sauces with the meats listed below. Guaranteed successful barbecuing!

Indoor Method:

Chicken: Brush 2 split broilers (2½ pounds each) with salad oil; place on broiler pan, skin-side down, 6 inches from heat.* Cook 15 minutes on each side. Brush with sauce; cook 30 minutes more or until chicken is tender, turning and brushing with sauce every 5 minutes. 4 servings.
*For gas broiler, follow manufacturer's directions.

Frankfurter: Slit 1 pound frankfurters. Broil 4 inches from heat for 10 minutes, turning and brushing with sauce. Serve on toasted frankfurter buns with remaining sauce. 4 to 5 servings.

Hamburger: Season 2 pounds ground beef with 1 teaspoon salt and dash pepper; shape into 8 patties. Broil 4 inches from heat for 15 minutes or until desired doneness, turning and brushing with sauce every 5 minutes. Serve on toasted hamburger buns with remaining sauce. 8 servings.

Sparerib: In large heavy pan, cover 4 pounds spareribs, cut in serving-size pieces, with water. Simmer 1 hour; drain. Place ribs on broiler pan. Broil 6 inches from heat* for 30 minutes, turning and brushing with sauce every 5 minutes. 4 servings.
*For gas broiler, follow manufacturer's directions.

Steak: Place 2-pound sirloin steak (about 1-inch thick) on broiler pan; brush with sauce. Broil 4 inches from heat for 4 to 5 minutes. Turn; brush with sauce. Broil 4 minutes more or until desired doneness. Heat remaining sauce; serve with steak. 4 to 6 servings.

Outdoor Method:

Chicken: Brush 2 split broilers (2½ pounds each) with salad oil; place on grill, skin-side up, about 6 inches above single layer of glowing coals. Cook 15 minutes on each side. Brush with sauce; cook 30 minutes more or until chicken is tender, turning and brushing with sauce every 5 minutes. 4 servings.

Frankfurter: Slit 1 pound frankfurters. Place on grill 4 inches above glowing coals. Cook, turning and brushing with sauce until browned. Heat remaining sauce; serve with frankfurters. 4 to 5 servings.

Hamburger: To prepare hamburgers, see Indoor Method. Place hamburgers on grill 4 inches above glowing coals. Cook 5 minutes brushing with sauce. Turn; continue brushing with sauce. Cook 5 minutes more or until desired doneness. 8 servings.

Sparerib: Precook spareribs following Indoor Method. Place spareribs on grill 6 inches above glowing coals. Cook 30 minutes, turning and brushing with sauce every 5 minutes. 4 servings.

Steak: Place 2-pound sirloin steak (about 1-inch thick) on grill 4 inches above glowing coals. Cook 5 minutes, brushing with sauce. Turn; continue brushing with sauce. Cook 5 minutes more or until desired doneness. Heat remaining sauce; serve with steak. 4 to 6 servings.

Chicken-Shrimp Kabobs, Curry Sauce

¼ cup chopped onion
1 tablespoon curry powder
2 tablespoons butter or margarine
1 can (10½ ounces) condensed
    chicken broth

4 teaspoons cornstarch
½ cup currant jelly
1 tablespoon lime juice

In saucepan, cook onion with curry in butter until tender. Remove from heat. Add remaining ingredients. Cook over low heat, stirring until thickened. Serve as barbecue sauce for Chicken-Shrimp Kabobs.

Chicken-Shrimp Kabobs: Prepare sauce. On 4 skewers arrange alternately: 1 whole chicken breast (about 1 pound), split, skinned, and boned, cut into 8 strips; 8 large raw shrimps (about ½ pound), cleaned; 8 green pepper squares (1-inch); 8 cherry tomatoes. 4 servings.

Indoor Method: Broil about 4 inches from heat 15 minutes or until done, turning and brushing with sauce every 5 minutes. Heat remaining sauce; serve with kabobs.

Outdoor Method: Brush kabobs lightly with salad oil. Place on grill 4 inches above glowing coals; cook 15 minutes or until done, turning and brushing with sauce every 5 minutes. Heat remaining sauce; serve with kabobs.

Company Chicken Cook-out

1 can (10½ ounces) condensed
 cream of mushroom soup
1 can (10½ ounces) condensed
 onion soup
½ cup ketchup
¼ cup salad oil

¼ cup vinegar
2 large cloves garlic, minced
2 tablespoons brown sugar
1 tablespoon Worcestershire
⅛ teaspoon hot pepper sauce
4 split broilers (2½ pounds each)

In saucepan, combine all ingredients except chicken. Cover; cook over low heat about 15 minutes. Stir now and then. Brush split broilers with salad oil; place on grill, skin-side up, about 6 inches above single layer of glowing coals. Cook 15 minutes on each side. Brush with sauce; cook 30 minutes more or until chicken is tender, turning and brushing with sauce every 5 minutes. 8 servings.

❋ Ribs with Apricot Barbecue Sauce

½ cup chopped onion
1 large clove garlic, minced
2 tablespoons salad oil
1 can (10½ ounces) condensed
 beef broth

1 cup apricot preserves
 (12-ounce jar)
¼ cup lemon juice
4 teaspoons soy sauce

Brush grill with oil before cooking. Meat should be at room temperature. Use marinades to flavor and tenderize less expensive cuts of meats and poultry. Keep the fare simple but good. Create an informal but attractive setting.

In saucepan, cook onion and garlic in oil until onion is tender. Add remaining ingredients. Cover; cook over low heat 15 minutes. Stir now and then. Serve as barbecue sauce for spareribs, following Indoor Method p. 112. Reduce broiling time to 20 minutes.

Lamb Chops Polynesian

1 can (10½ ounces) condensed
 onion soup
¼ cup drained crushed pineapple
2 tablespoons brown sugar
1 teaspoon cornstarch
⅛ teaspoon ground allspice

⅛ teaspoon ground coriander
8 lamb or veal chops, 1-inch
 thick (about 2 to 2½
 pounds)
Salad oil

In saucepan, combine soup, pineapple, brown sugar, cornstarch, allspice, and coriander. Cook, stirring until thickened. Brush chops lightly with oil. Place on grill 4 inches above glowing coals. Cook for 10 minutes, brushing with sauce. Turn; continue brushing with sauce. Cook 10 minutes more or until desired doneness. Heat remaining sauce; serve with chops. 4 servings.

Zippy Barbecue Sauce tops Chicken on the grill . . .
to be served with roasting ears for a picnic to please!

Tony's Barbecued Burgers

1 can (10¾ ounces) condensed
    tomato soup
1 can (2 ounces) mushrooms,
    drained and chopped

¼ cup chopped onion
1 small clove garlic, minced
1 teaspoon oregano, crushed

In saucepan, combine all ingredients. Cover; cook over low heat 10 minutes. Stir now and then. Thin with water, if desired. Serve as barbecue sauce for hamburgers, following Indoor Method page 112.

Saucy Beef Kabobs

1 pound beef sirloin cut in 1-inch
    cubes (16 pieces)
½ cup dry red wine
1 medium clove garlic, minced
⅛ teaspoon basil, crushed
1 tablespoon butter or margarine
1 can (10½ ounces) condensed
    golden mushroom soup

¼ cup ketchup
12 pieces green pepper
    (1-inch), parboiled 2
    minutes
12 cherry tomatoes
Salad Oil

In deep bowl, combine meat and wine; refrigerate 2 hours. Drain, reserving wine. In saucepan, cook garlic and basil in butter; stir in soup, wine, and ketchup. Cook over low heat for 5 minutes. Stir now and then. Arrange alternately on 4 skewers: beef, pepper, and tomatoes; brush lightly with oil. Place on grill 4 inches above glowing coals. Cook for 12 to 18 minutes turning and brushing frequently with sauce. Heat remaining sauce; serve over kabobs. 4 servings.

Beef on a Spit

1 can (10½ ounces) condensed
    onion soup
½ soup can water
1 tablespoon bleu cheese,
    crumbled

3 to 4-pound top quality beef
    rotisserie roast

In shallow baking dish, combine soup, water, and cheese; add beef. Marinate at room temperature for 2 hours; turn once. Save marinade. Mount and balance beef on spit. Insert meat thermometer into beef. Roast 1½ hours or until 130° F. (rare) on meat thermometer following oven manufacturer's directions. In saucepan, heat marinade until cheese is melted; stir now and then. Thicken with 1 tablespoon flour, if desired. Serve with meat. 6 to 8 servings.

Rotisserie Beef and Big Red Sauce

2 cans (10¾ ounces each)
    condensed tomato soup
2 tablespoons honey
2 tablespoons wine vinegar

1 medium clove garlic, minced
¼ teaspoon leaf thyme, crushed
3 to 4-pound top quality beef
    rotisserie roast

In saucepan, combine all ingredients except roast. Cover; cook over low heat 10 minutes. Stir now and then. Mount and balance beef on spit. Insert meat thermometer into beef. Roast 1½ hours or until 130° F. (rare) on meat thermometer following oven manufacturer's directions. Brush often with sauce the last 30 minutes. Heat remaining sauce; serve with meat. 6 to 8 servings.

Outdoor Method: Mount and balance beef on spit. Insert meat thermometer into beef. Place foil drip pan under meat to catch drippings. Place in barbecue rotisserie over glowing coals. Roast 1½ hours or until 130°F. (rare) on meat thermometer. Brush often with sauce the last 30 minutes. Heat remaining sauce; serve with meat.

London Broil Exceptionale

1 can (10¾ ounces) condensed
    tomato soup
⅓ cup Burgundy or other dry
    red wine
2 tablespoons finely chopped
    ripe olives

1 small clove garlic, minced
1 tablespoon finely chopped
    onion
1½ pound flank steak, scored

In shallow baking dish, combine all ingredients except steak. Add steak. Marinate at room temperature 1 hour turning once. Transfer steak to broiler pan. In saucepan, cook marinade covered over low heat 10 minutes; stir now and then. Broil steak 4 inches from heat about 4 minutes on each side or until desired doneness, brushing with sauce. Heat remaining sauce; serve with steak. 6 servings.

Outdoor Method: Proceed as above. Cook 4 inches above glowing coals 5 minutes on each side, brushing with sauce. Serve with remaining sauce.

Oniony Barbecued Burgers

⅓ cup finely chopped celery
1 tablespoon butter or margarine
1 tablespoon flour
1 can (10½ ounces) condensed
    onion soup

¼ cup ketchup
¼ cup water
1 tablespoon horseradish
¼ teaspoon Worcestershire

In saucepan, cook celery in butter until tender. Add flour. Gradually stir in remaining ingredients. Cook, stirring until thickened. Serve as barbecue sauce for hamburgers or steak, following Indoor or Outdoor Methods pages 112 and 113.

SAUCES

The triumph of many of our most favored dishes may be attributed to the selection of the sauce. Sauces enhance many foods by imparting desirable flavors to them, and by making them more attractive.

Contrary to the belief of many cooks who have tried to master the art of sauce preparation, however, there is no sorcery involved. Today sauce-making is quite easy in contrast to what Brillat-Savarin wrote some years ago: "One can learn to cook, and one can be taught to roast, but a good sauce-maker is a genius born, not made." In the realm of *haute cuisine*, particularly that developed by the French, the intricate and lengthy technique of making refined sauces was not easily acquired.

But now, happily you have superb sauces at your fingertips in double-rich, double-thick condensed soups.

These soups have the delicate extra seasoning and ingredients that make them excellent sauces as they come from the can. For example, cream of chicken or cream of mushroom which go so well with many meats and vegetables. Golden mushroom soup blends the elegance of wine and herbs with beef stock, resulting in mushroom sauce par excellence.

With the repertoire of basic soup-sauces and many savory variations, you are prepared to offer family and guests the best of these specialties.

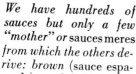

We have hundreds of sauces but only a few "mother" or sauces meres from which the others derive: brown (sauce espagnole) and white (bechamel) are the two great basics.

❋ Bearnaise Sauce

2 tablespoons chopped shallots
   or onions
¼ teaspoon tarragon, crushed
2 tablespoons butter or margarine
½ cup Sauterne or other dry
   white wine

½ teaspoon tarragon vinegar
1 can (10½ ounces) condensed
   cream of celery soup
2 egg yolks

In saucepan, cook shallots and tarragon in butter until shallots are tender. Add wine and vinegar; simmer a few minutes. Remove from heat. Stir in soup and egg yolks. Cook over low heat, stirring constantly until thickened. Makes 1⅔ cups sauce. Serve over sliced cooked beef, or broiled fish.

❋ Souper Gravy
For beef, chicken, pork, potatoes, noodles, or rice

1 can (10½ ounces) condensed
   cream of celery, chicken,
   mushroom or golden
   mushroom soup

¼ to ⅓ cup water
2 to 4 tablespoons drippings
   or butter

When preparing gravy for roast or fried meat, remove meat from pan and pour off and measure drippings. Pour can of soup into pan; stir well to loosen browned bits. Blend in water and drippings. Heat; stir often. Makes 1½ cups gravy.

Stroganoff Sauce

¼ cup chopped onion
½ teaspoon paprika
2 tablespoons butter or margarine

1 can (10½ ounces) condensed
   golden mushroom soup
¼ cup sour cream

In saucepan, cook onion with paprika in butter until tender. Stir in soup and sour cream. Heat; stir now and then. Makes 1½ cups sauce. Serve over sliced cooked beef, hamburgers, noodles, potatoes, or rice.

Three delectable fool-proof sauces: Hollandaise, Chasseur and Bearnaise. Each adorns a treasured food and is prepared in minutes with condensed soup, a joy to many cooks.

SAUCE CHART

✳ *Basic Cream Sauce* *(similar to Bechamel and Veloute)*

Serve with cooked vegetables.

Combine 1 can condensed cream of celery or chicken or mushroom soup with ⅓ to ½ cup milk. Heat; stir. Makes 1½ cups.

Variations:

✳ *Hollandaise Sauce*

To Basic Cream Sauce add 2 tablespoons each butter and lemon juice and 2 egg yolks, slightly beaten. Simmer until just thickened (about 5 minutes), stirring constantly. Makes 1¾ cups. Serve with cooked vegetables or fish.

Mornay Sauce

To Basic Cream Sauce add ½ cup shredded natural Swiss cheese, 2 tablespoons grated Parmesan cheese. Heat until cheese melts; stir often. Makes 1½ cups. Serve over cooked meats, poultry, fish, vegetables, or poached eggs.

Onion Sauce

Cook ½ cup chopped onion in 2 tablespoons butter until tender. Stir in ingredients for Basic Cream Sauce. Serve over cooked meats, fish, or vegetables.

✳ *Sour Cream Sauce*

Cook ¼ cup chopped onion in 1 tablespoon butter until tender. Stir in Basic Cream Sauce, substituting ½ cup sour cream for milk in Basic Cream Sauce recipe, and ⅛ teaspoon paprika. Heat; stir. Makes 2 cups. Serve with cooked noodles, meats, or poultry.

✳ *Basic Tomato Sauce*

Serve with cooked fish and meat.

Combine 1 can (10¾ ounces) condensed tomato soup with 2 tablespoons water. Heat; stir. Makes 1¼ cups.

Variations:

To Basic Tomato Sauce add *any one* of the following before heating:

⅛ teaspoon crushed basil or oregano.

¼ teaspoon crushed dill leaves.

1 tablespoon capers.

2 tablespoons chopped parsley or ripe olives.

1 teaspoon prepared mustard.

Substitute sour cream for water.

2 teaspoons Worcestershire or horseradish.

❈ Basic Cheddar Cheese Sauce

Serve with cooked fish, meat, omelets, poultry, or vegetables.

Combine 1 can condensed Cheddar cheese soup with ¼ to ⅓ cup milk. Heat; stir. Makes 1½ cups.

Variations:

To Basic Cheese Sauce add *any one* of the following before heating:

1 tablespoon chili sauce or ketchup.

2 tablespoons chopped parsley.

Generous dash crushed dried dill leaves or nutmeg.

Substitute sour cream for milk.

❈ Basic Golden Mushroom Sauce

Serve with cooked meats, noodles, potatoes, poultry, or rice.

Combine 1 can condensed golden mushroom soup with ⅓ cup water. Heat; stir. Makes 1½ cups.

Variations:

Bordelaise Sauce
Cook ¼ cup chopped onion or shallots in 2 tablespoons butter. Add ¼ cup dry red wine; simmer a few minutes. Stir in Golden Mushroom Sauce, 1 tablespoon chopped parsley. Heat; stir. Makes 2 cups. Serve over cooked meats, poultry, or vegetables.

Chasseur Sauce
Cook 2 tablespoons sliced green onion or chopped shallots with dash crushed tarragon in 1 tablespoon butter until onion is tender. Add ¼ cup dry white wine; simmer a few minutes. Stir in Golden Mushroom Sauce, 2 tablespoons chopped canned tomato, and 1 tablespoon minced parsley. Heat; stir. Makes 1⅔ cups. Serve with cooked meats or poultry.

Espagnole Sauce
Cook 1 slice bacon; remove and crumble. Add ⅓ cup chopped onion, 1 small bay leaf, and ⅛ teaspoon crushed leaf thyme to drippings; cook until onion is tender. Stir in Golden Mushroom Sauce, ⅓ cup tomato juice, and reserved bacon. Heat; stir. Makes 2 cups. Serve with cooked meats, poultry, or vegetables.

Herb Sauce
Cook ⅓ cup chopped onion or shallots in 2 tablespoons butter until tender. Add ¼ cup dry white wine; simmer a few minutes. Stir in Golden Mushroom Sauce, 1 tablespoon chopped parsley, and generous dash each crushed chervil and tarragon. Heat; stir. Makes 2 cups. Serve over cooked meats, poultry, or vegetables.

Madeira Sauce
Simmer ¼ cup Madeira wine a few minutes. Stir in Golden Mushroom Sauce. Heat; stir. Makes 1⅔ cups. Serve over cooked meats or poultry.

Lyonnaise Sauce
Cook 1 cup chopped onion in 3 tablespoons butter until tender. Add ¼ cup dry white wine; simmer a few minutes. Stir in Golden Mushroom Sauce. Heat; stir. Makes 2 cups. Serve with cooked meats, poultry, or vegetables.

ENTERTAINING
for Family and Friends

Social gatherings have essentially the same purpose at your house and mine—to express the spirit of hospitality. The pleasant memory of the guest is the hostess' reward. A common bond of all of us is this desire to welcome family and friends with good taste and versatility. The occasion may include a few or many persons, may be simple or elegant, with little or much fine fare.

To maintain hospitable standards in today's hectic world, however, requires some forethought. If you're an experienced hostess, you may well know the problems of coping with your various roles as shopper, planner, cook and director. If you're less experienced, perhaps a bride, you may just now be confronted with creating, planning and performing the varied chores attendant on your new status. All of us, however, welcome proven ideas and imaginative suggestions to make our social events distinctive and individual.

In offering here some helpful hints, creative menus and reliable recipes for a variety of occasions, the aim is to inspire not restrict. For each individual will interpret them in her own style. By simplifying your approach, however, you'll find that hospitality need be neither hectic nor haphazard.

Plan the event, organize your resources, take advantage of the excellent and varied convenience foods the modern world affords, and, above all, prepare as much of the fare as possible beforehand. You'll be calm and composed—no furrowed brow—when your guests arrive.

Planning the Party
What Is The Occasion? There are many reasons and times for entertaining. It may be a party to welcome neighbors, celebrate a birthday, greet old

friends, salute a co-worker. To vary the usual luncheons and dinners, dream up a theme to make the party memorable. Invite guests to come in costume, perhaps for a Mexican Fiesta or plan a Continental Buffet.

What Kind Of A Party? Before deciding the kind of party and how many persons to invite, consider your entertaining facilities. The seating and serving space will influence the number.

The Menu: In selecting the menu, plan on dishes which you know. Choose foods which can be partially or completely prepared ahead. In general, it is advisable to avoid exotic foods. A simple, but good, menu is often preferable to the more elaborate one.

Service: The best and easiest way to serve company depends on your home and equipment. Perhaps you find buffet parties go most smoothly; however, this requires trays or tray tables. Some find it handier to use the traditional "at table" approach with the host doing the honors in serving the main course to each guest while the hostess adds accompaniments.

Preparing The Food: Cook beforehand as much of the menu as possible. Some dishes can be frozen well in advance. Others will keep overnight in the refrigerator. Leave only what is absolutely necessary for the day of the party. Calculate the cooking times for any dishes which have to be done after guests arrive so everything is ready at once. Be sure you have not counted on using one oven for dishes which take different temperatures.

The Day of the Party

In The Morning: Check all the details of the party. Has the ice been made? Is there a place for coats? Have the necessary serving dishes and utensils been gathered?

At The Party: After the guests arrive, relax and enjoy yourself, while you are keeping an eye on what is going on. Try to serve the meal on schedule. If unexpected crises arise, take them in good stride. Above all, plan so you can enjoy your guests and so they enjoy your hospitality.

The following menus give a variety of suggestions for brunches, luncheons, and dinners. Asterisks mark the menu items for which there are recipes.

Brunch Elegante

In New Orleans, 'tis the late-morning custom to dine elegantly and leisurely at brunch, beginning with a favorite "eye-opener" and concluding with hot strong coffee. The meal may be enjoyed on a flower-decorated patio or inside. But guests will welcome a gay and pretty setting. For a color theme, use a pastel cloth or mats and napkins. The fruit course can be a spectacular centerpiece if you serve it in a hollowed small watermelon; dice the pink melon to mix with the oranges and berries; then heap in the green shell. Or you may prefer to serve individual halves of cantaloupe filled with other fruits. If you serve Eggs Benedict, you may want to use toasted English muffin halves as the base. Or if the chicken dish is your choice, remember the excellent frozen patty shells. The regal cake winds up the repast in fitting style and is not too sweet.

Chilled Fresh Orange Slices with Berries

Eggs Benedict* or Chicken and Eggs Francoise*

Angelfood Cake with Chocolate Glaze

Milk or Coffee

❋ *Eggs Benedict*

1 can (10½ ounces) condensed
    cream of celery, chicken, or
    mushroom soup
⅓ cup milk

6 thin slices ham, fried
6 slices buttered toast
6 eggs, poached
1 tablespoon minced parsley

In saucepan, blend soup and milk. Heat; stir now and then. Meanwhile, place a slice of ham on each slice of toast; top with a poached egg. Pour sauce over eggs. Garnish with parsley. 6 servings.

Chicken and Eggs Francoise

1 can (2 ounces) mushroom
    buttons, drained
⅛ teaspoon thyme, crushed
4 tablespoons butter or margarine
1 can (10½ ounces) condensed
    cream of celery soup
¾ cup light cream or milk

1 cup cubed, cooked chicken
2 tablespoons chopped pimiento
4 eggs, slightly beaten
¼ teaspoon salt
4 patty shells
Chopped parsley

In saucepan, brown mushrooms with thyme in 2 tablespoons butter until tender. Add soup, ½ cup cream, chicken, and pimiento. Heat; stir now and then. Meanwhile, combine eggs, salt, and ¼ cup cream. In skillet, gently scramble eggs in 2 tablespoons butter. Layer eggs and creamed chicken in patty shells. Garnish with parsley. 4 servings.

Continental Luncheon

In Rome, Vienna, Boston or Omaha, a week-day luncheon is a happy occasion for women friends to gather and enjoy a few hours of leisure and good talk. Welcome your guests to an imaginative setting using pretty linens, china, and an artistic centerpiece. For canapes, place a slice of cucumber on each buttered round of white bread; garnish with a dab of mayonnaise and chopped chives; refrigerate. The crepes can be prepared and frozen beforehand. Thaw and fill before the party. Sprinkle the tomatoes with oil, vinegar, fresh herbs, salt and pepper; refrigerate. The souffle can be made the day before.

Cucumber Canapes with Cups of Hot Beef Broth

Shrimp and Ham in Patty Shells* or Crepes a la Reine*

Tomato Slices Vinaigrette

Cold Lemon Souffle

Café au Lait

❋ Shrimp and Ham in Patty Shells

1 cup ham strips
2 cups sliced mushrooms
   (about ½ pound)
1 medium clove garlic, minced
¼ cup butter or margarine

2 cans (10½ ounces each)
   condensed cream of chicken soup
½ cup light cream
2 cups cooked shrimp
¼ cup chopped parsley
6 patty shells

In saucepan, brown ham and cook mushrooms and garlic in butter. Stir in soup and cream. Add shrimp and parsley. Heat; stir now and then. Serve in patty shells. 6 servings.

Crepes a la Reine

Filling and sauce:

1½ cups chopped mushrooms
   (about ¼ pound)
¼ cup chopped onion
⅛ teaspoon thyme, crushed
¼ cup butter or margarine
1 can (10½ ounces) condensed
   cream of chicken soup

1½ cups diced cooked chicken
¼ teaspoon salt
Dash pepper
¼ cup light cream
2 tablespoons Sauterne or
   other dry white wine

Crepes:

⅓ cup flour
3 eggs

⅔ cup milk
Dash salt

In skillet, brown mushrooms and cook onion with thyme in butter until tender. Stir in ¼ cup soup, chicken, salt, and pepper. Heat; stir now and then. Meanwhile, in saucepan, combine remaining soup, cream, and Sauterne. Heat; stir now and then. In bowl, combine ingredients for crepes; beat until smooth. In hot, lightly buttered, small skillet, cook 8 crepes (6-inch diameter) on both sides, using about 2 tablespoons batter for each. Tilt pan slightly to get evenly thin crepes. Hold on heated plate. Place 3 to 4 tablespoons filling on each crepe; roll up. Pour sauce over and serve immediately. 4 servings.

For a Continental Luncheon feature Shrimp and Ham in Patty Shells. *Perfect finale, cold lemon souffle.*

Soup and Sandwich Times

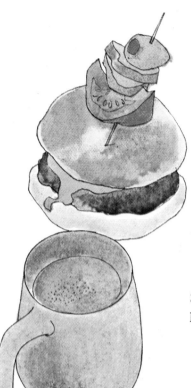

Teen-Agers' Pre-Shopping Lunch

Give added pizazz to the usual without going too unusual; toss in the convenience of out-of-hand eating and you have the necessary formula for feeding a teen.

Mugs of Green Pea Soup or Chicken Vegetable Soup
Party-Burgers*
Orange Sherbet

Party-Burgers

Prepare Cheeseburgers as usual. Top each with a kabob of nibblers—pickle chips, olives, tomato wedges.

Lunch for Grandmother's Friends

Set a frilly table complete with the best china, and tea roses in a crystal vase to complement a fancy menu.

Cups of Hot Tomato Chantilly*
Minced Chicken and Salmon
Finger Sandwiches
Cranberry Relish on Lettuce
Brownies a la Mode
Hot Tea

Tomato Chantilly

1 can (10¾ ounces) condensed   *Whipped cream*
   tomato soup   *Nutmeg*
1 soup can water

In saucepan, combine soup and water. Heat; stir now and then. Meanwhile, place about 1 teaspoon whipped cream in each cup or mug; sprinkle with nutmeg. Pour hot soup over; serve immediately. 3 servings.

Golfers' Get-Together

Whether your "pro" gets the trophy or finishes last in the day's tournament, he'll know he's got a winner when you offer him this man-pleasing reward.

Cream of Potato Soup or Clam Chowder with Croutons
Reuben Sandwiches
(Corned Beef, Sauerkraut, and Swiss Cheese on Rye Bread)
Pickles and Radishes
Tray of Assorted Cookies and Fruit
Iced Coffee

Soup and Salad Times

A Hot-Weather Lunch

Refresh your salad days with a cup or bowl of chilled soup eaten alfresco. Invite the back-fence neighbors over to make lunch an occasion.

Chilled Cream of Asparagus Soup with Sour Cream
Chicken-Orange Salad in Orange Shells*
Crusty Rolls
Nut Cookies
Milk or Iced Coffee

Chicken-Orange Salad

Toss together cooked cubed chicken, orange sections, and celery with a light dressing.

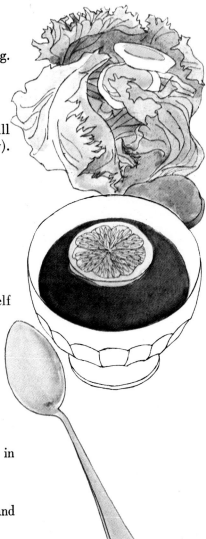

Christmas Luncheon

Greet guests in the living room with a cup of warming soup to "sip and spoon" (it will keep hot in a chafing dish or in a handsome heat-proof casserole on a warming tray).

Cups of Chicken Rice or Turkey Vegetable Soup
Ribbon Aspic* *(see index)*
Mince Pie or Fruit Cake and Ice Cream
Hot Spiced Tea or Coffee

An Easy Sunday Lunch

To fill the bill for a day of relaxation—make the salads a day ahead and add shelf handy canned items.

Cups of Black Bean Soup with Lemon Slices
Ham-and-Egg Salad*
Toast or Melba Toast Rounds
Rice Pudding*
Milk or Hot Coffee

Ham-and-Egg Salad

Mix strips of ham with sliced hard-cooked eggs, celery, and mayonnaise. Serve in lettuce cups.

Rice Pudding

Buy prepared pudding. Spoon into sherbet glasses; top with strawberry jam and chopped pecans.

131

**Old Fashioned
Vegetable Soup**

German Sauerbraten*

**Hot Noodles with Poppy-
seeds or Hot Potato Puffs**

Cabbage-Carrot Slaw

Pumpernickel Slices

Warm Apple Turnovers

Cheddar Cheese

Cold Beer

Coffee

Herbed Tomato Slush* or
Consomme Parfait*
(see index)

Quick Chicken Divan*
(see index)

Spiced Apricot Garnish

Melba Toast

Chocolate Bavarian

Coffee

Autumn-Winter Luncheon for Men

A gathering of men for any occasion is an opportunity to enjoy the German spirit of *Gemutlichkeit*, a convivial celebration with good food and drinks. You can prepare this fare and set the whole meal, except dessert, on a buffet to let each man help himself. The host can ladle the soup into mugs or cups from a tureen or bowl. Slice the meat in the kitchen beforehand. Use the potato puffs and turnovers that come frozen to be heated in the oven.

German Sauerbraten

4-pound rump roast
1 can (10½ ounces) condensed
 onion soup
¾ cup wine vinegar
½ cup water
3 medium bay leaves

6 whole peppercorns
10 whole cloves
2 tablespoons shortening
¼ cup sugar
½ cup crumbled ginger snaps
 (about 7)

Place meat in deep bowl. Combine soup, vinegar, water, bay, peppercorns, and cloves; pour over meat. Cover, refrigerate for 2 days, turning meat twice each day. Remove meat from marinade. In large heavy pan, brown meat in shortening; pour off fat. Stir in marinade. Cover; cook over low heat 2½ hours or until tender. Remove meat from pan; keep warm. Skim fat from gravy; remove bay, peppercorns, and cloves. Stir in sugar and ginger snaps. Cook until thickened, stirring. Serve with meat. 6 to 8 servings.

The Committee Luncheon

This menu is a delightful one to serve buffet-style. Fill sherbet glasses or cups with Herbed Tomato Slush or Consomme Parfait; garnish with yogurt and chopped chives, or watercress or dill; refrigerate. Pass to guests before the meal. The attractive chicken dish can be partially prepared beforehand and baked after the guests arrive. For decor, feature the colors of nature (which are Danish favorites), green and blue with white. Serve luncheon in keeping with the Danish *Velbekomme,* "May this meal become you well."

Herbed Tomato Slush

1 tablespoon finely chopped onion
⅛ teaspoon marjoram, crushed
⅛ teaspoon tarragon, crushed
1 tablespoon butter or margarine

1 can (10¾ ounces) condensed
 tomato soup
1 soup can water
1 tablespoon lemon juice

In saucepan, cook onion with marjoram and tarragon in butter until tender. Stir in remaining ingredients. Pour into shallow pan. Freeze until partially frozen (about 3 hours); stir a few times. Break up ice with fork; spoon into sherbet glasses or bowls. 4 servings.

Bring-the-Children Brunch

At a brunch after church or a lazy morning, parents and the younger set can all relax. The children may sit together at a small table, prettily decorated with paper appointments, while the grown-ups dine elsewhere. First serve juices and coffee from a cart as a welcoming note. Mix and shape the meat beforehand and bake after the guests arrive (takes only 20 minutes). Have the prepared vegetable platter (cucumbers, green peppers, carrots and celery) in the refrigerator.

Chilled Fruit Juices
Beef 'n Frank
Wagon Wheel*
Raw Vegetable Platter—
Mustard, Mayonnaise
Hot Buttered Toast
Jam   Jelly
Sugared Doughnuts
Cold Milk   Coffee

Beef 'n Frank Wagon Wheel

1 can (10¾ ounces) condensed
   tomato soup
1½ pounds ground beef
1 teaspoon salt
1½ teaspoons chili powder
6 frankfurters, split

½ cup chopped onion
2 tablespoons
   butter or margarine
½ cup shredded process
   cheese
Grated Parmesan cheese

Place a double layer of foil on cookie sheet. Mix thoroughly ⅓ cup soup, beef, salt, and 1 teaspoon chili powder; pat out firmly into 11-inch circle about ½ inch thick on foil. Turn up edges of foil to catch fat. Firmly press frankfurters, cut side up, into meat in spoke fashion. In saucepan, cook onion with remaining chili in butter until tender; stir in remaining soup; spread over meat. Bake at 450°F. for 15 minutes. Spoon off fat. Sprinkle with cheeses; bake until melted. 6 servings.

Indoor-Outdoor Summertime Lunch

On a hot Sunday or summer holiday, some of us wish to dine leisurely outdoors but others prefer the comfort of a cooler indoor party. For either, summertime fare is superb. The cool Vichyssoise and aspic can be already prepared in the refrigerator. For the asparagus, saute ½ cup slivered almonds in ½ cup butter until golden; add 2 tablespoons lemon juice, salt and pepper; pour over hot cooked asparagus (2 pounds raw). Have the dessert ready in the refrigerator.

Vichyssoise*
(see index)
Calico Beef Aspic*
Asparagus Amandine
Hot Biscuits
Butter   Marmalade
Fresh Pineapple Wedges
Coffee—Iced or Hot

Calico Beef Aspic

1 can (10½ ounces) condensed
   beef broth
1 package (3 ounces)
   lemon-flavored gelatin
½ cup cold water
1 tablespoon grated onion

1 tablespoon vinegar
Dash salt
Dash pepper
1 cup diced cooked beef
⅓ cup diced red apple
2 tablespoons sliced celery

In saucepan, bring beef broth to a boil. Add gelatin; stir to dissolve. Add water, onion, vinegar, salt, and pepper. Chill until slightly thickened. Fold in remaining ingredients. Pour into a 3-cup mold. Chill until firm (about 4 hours). Garnish with hard-cooked egg wedges. 4 servings.

Memorable Christmas Dinner

An important consideration for Christmas dinner is to plan one which will leave you time to enjoy the day's festivities. For the merry yuletide feast is a happy event to be shared with family and friends. Prepare much of the menu beforehand. Buy canned oyster stew. Have the salad ready in the refrigerator. The acorn squash offers a change from the standard potatoes. Dessert may be pretty ice cream balls, frozen and ready to be served with bourbon-flavored or plain egg nog sauce, or the more traditional plum pudding which can be purchased.

Stuffed Turkey with Holiday Sauce

6 slices bacon
1 cup sliced celery
½ cup chopped onion
1 package (8 ounces) herb-seasoned stuffing mix
2 cups coarse cornbread crumbs
1 can (10½ ounces) condensed chicken broth
1 egg, slightly beaten
10-pound turkey
1 can (10½ ounces) condensed cream of mushroom soup
½ cup whole berry cranberry sauce
¼ cup orange juice

In skillet, cook bacon until crisp; remove and crumble. Pour off all but 2 tablespoons drippings. Cook celery and onion in drippings until tender. Toss lightly with stuffing mix, crumbs, broth, and egg. Fill cavity of turkey loosely with stuffing. Truss; place in roasting pan. Cover with aluminum foil. Roast at 325° F. for about 4 hours (25 minutes per pound or until tender). Uncover last hour to brown. Remove turkey to serving platter. Skim fat from drippings; add remaining ingredients. Heat; stir to loosen browned bits. 8 servings.

✻ Glazed Carrots and Brussels Sprouts
Pictured on front cover

1 pound carrots, cut in 1½-inch pieces
2 packages (10 ounces each) frozen Brussels sprouts
2 tablespoons chopped onion
2 tablespoons butter or margarine
1 can (10½ ounces) condensed consomme
⅓ cup apple juice
2 teaspoons lemon juice
2 tablespoons cornstarch
1 tablespoon brown sugar
Generous dash ground clove

Cook carrots and Brussels sprouts; drain. Meanwhile, in saucepan, cook onion in butter until tender. Add remaining ingredients. Cook, stirring until thickened. Combine with hot vegetables. 8 servings.

This Christmas Dinner coasts into the spotlight carrying a luscious trio of buttery Oyster Stew, *squash and* Stuffed Turkey with Holiday Sauce.

Pork Dinner for New Year's

The world's oldest holiday, and the only one celebrated by all peoples everywhere, is most happily spent mixing convivially with friends or relatives. You may wish to promote this harmonious spirit by entertaining with an inviting dinner during the day or in the evening. It is a pleasing variation to include dishes which are not traditional for the "Twelve Days of Christmas." This pork dinner is such an innovation.

Bullshot

Fill an old fashioned glass with ice cubes. Add 1 ounce vodka. Pour in 4 ounces (½ cup) undiluted beef broth. Garnish with slice of lemon. 1 serving.

Bully Scotch Sipper

3½ ounces condensed beef broth   *1 ounce Scotch*

Fill an 8-ounce old fashioned glass with ice cubes. Add beef broth and Scotch. Stir. Garnish with lemon peel. Serve with celery stick stirrer. 1 serving.

❈ Party Cheese Log

*1 can (11½ ounces) condensed
    bean with bacon soup*
*4 cups (1 pound) shredded
    sharp Cheddar cheese*
½ cup finely chopped onion

2 tablespoons Worcestershire
1 teaspoon basil, crushed
1 medium clove garlic, minced
½ teaspoon hot pepper sauce
½ cup finely chopped parsley

In large bowl, stir all ingredients except parsley until well blended. On waxed paper, shape mixture into log (10x2 inches). Chill 2 hours. Roll in parsley. Serve with chips and crackers.

Glazed Pork Loin

4-pound loin of pork
⅓ cup chopped celery
1 tablespoon butter or margarine
*1 can (10½ ounces) condensed
    consomme*

2 tablespoons lemon juice
2 tablespoons brown sugar
1 tablespoon cornstarch
¼ teaspoon dry mustard
Generous dash cinnamon

In roasting pan, roast meat fat side up at 325°F. for about 2½ hours (35 to 40 minutes per pound or 170°F. on meat thermometer). Meanwhile, in saucepan, cook celery in butter until tender; add remaining ingredients. Cook over low heat, stirring until thickened. During last 30 minutes of roasting time, brush roast frequently with sauce. Heat remaining sauce; serve with roast. 6 to 8 servings.

Festive Easter Dinner

With spring in the air and everyone in good spirits, the delights of Easter are many. A most enjoyable way of celebrating the holiday is with a pleasing Sunday dinner served at a festive table. Make a centerpiece of colored Easter eggs or with spring flowers. Perhaps the meal will precede or follow an indoor or outdoor egg hunt. Or, in the Greek tradition, begin the meal with the ancient custom of egg cracking. Each person tries to crack the tip of a hard-cooked egg held tightly in the hand of the person next to him. When all are cracked, best wishes are exchanged. This menu of familiar dishes can be enjoyed at leisure.

"V-8" Cocktail
Vegetable Juice
Curried Stuffed Eggs
Mint-glazed Leg of Lamb*
Scalloped Potatoes* or
Parsleyed New Potatoes
Buttered Fresh Broccoli
Lettuce with Herb Dressing
Hot Nut Muffins
Strawberry Ice Cream Pie

Mint-glazed Leg of Lamb

4 to 5-pound leg of lamb
¼ cup chopped onion
1 small clove garlic, minced
1 tablespoon butter or margarine
1 can (10½ ounces)
condensed consomme

½ cup mint-flavored
   apple jelly
5 teaspoons cornstarch
1 tablespoon lemon juice

Remove fell from lamb (parchment-like covering); trim excess fat. Place on rack in shallow baking dish, fat side up. Roast at 325°F. until done (30 to 35 minutes per pound or 175°F. on meat thermometer). Meanwhile, in saucepan, cook onion with garlic in butter until tender; add remaining ingredients. Cook over low heat, stirring until thickened. Brush lamb with sauce during last 30 minutes. Heat remaining sauce, serve with lamb. 4 to 6 servings.

❈ Scalloped Potatoes

1 can (10½ ounces) condensed
   cream of celery
   or mushroom soup
½ cup milk
¼ cup chopped parsley
Dash pepper

4 cups thinly sliced raw
   potatoes
1 small onion, thinly sliced
1 tablespoon
   butter or margarine
Dash paprika

Combine soup, milk, parsley, and pepper. In a buttered 1½-quart casserole, arrange alternate layers of potatoes, onion, and sauce. Dot top with butter; sprinkle with paprika. Cover; bake at 325°F. for 1½ hours. Uncover; bake 15 minutes more or until potatoes are done. 4 to 6 servings.

V. I. P. Dinner

On that special occasion when you wish to serve a sit-down dinner with gracious elegance and your best appointments, this menu matches the mood. For the decor, select a single color to accent in napkins and candles—perhaps royal blue. Use place cards, and attach a fresh flower blossom to each napkin. For salad, cook small carrots; chill; and cover with sour cream.

Chilled Minted Pea Soup
Recipe may be doubled

1 can (11¼ ounces) condensed
   green pea soup
1 soup can milk

¼ cup light cream
½ teaspoon dried mint flakes,
   crushed

Blend all ingredients. Chill at least 4 hours. 3 servings.

❋ Stuffed Beef Roll

1½ pounds round steak (about
   ¼ inch thick), trimmed
¼ pound ground veal
1 egg, slightly beaten
¼ cup small bread cubes
2 tablespoons grated Parmesan cheese
2 slices (2 ounces) salami,
   cut in strips
2 slices (2 ounces) Provolone
   cheese, cut in strips

2 hard-cooked eggs, sliced
2 tablespoons shortening
1 can (10¾ ounces)
   condensed tomato soup
½ cup water
½ cup chopped onion
¼ cup Burgundy or other
   dry red wine
1 medium clove garlic, minced
1 small bay leaf

Pound steak with meat hammer or edge of heavy saucer. Combine veal, egg, bread, and Parmesan cheese. Spread mixture evenly on steak to within 1 inch of edges. Press salami, Provolone cheese, and sliced eggs into meat mixture. Starting at narrow end, roll up; tuck in ends. Tie with string or fasten with skewers. In skillet, brown roll in shortening; pour off fat. Add remaining ingredients. Cover; cook over low heat 1 hour. Turn; cook 1 hour more. Stir now and then. 6 servings.

❋ Pilaf
Recipe may be doubled

½ cup fine egg noodles, broken
   in pieces
2 tablespoons butter or margarine

1 can (10½ ounces)
   condensed chicken broth
⅓ cup water
½ cup raw regular rice

In saucepan, brown noodles in butter; stir often. Add remaining ingredients. Bring to a boil; stir. Cover; cook over low heat 20 to 25 minutes or until liquid is absorbed. 3 to 4 servings.

Fun with Fondue

The serving of Beef Fondue Bourguignonne is a friendly meal with everyone seated around the cooking dish. Each person cooks the meat in hot oil in the fondue pot or chafing dish according to individual preference. Then the beef is dunked in one or more flavorful sauces. It is preferable to have long-handled forks for the cooking of the beef. You may vary the accompaniments as desired but they are generally light fare. Glasses of red wine often are served with the fondue.

Fondue Bourguignonne*
Assorted Sauces*
Individual Green Salads
French Bread
Melon with Lime or
Mint Ice Cream
Coffee

❋ *Fondue Bourguignonne*

1 can (10½ ounces) condensed
   cream of celery soup

2 pounds sirloin steak or filet
   mignon
Vegetable oil

Using soup, prepare any combination of sauces listed below. Cut meat into ¾-inch cubes; trim all fat. Refrigerate until 30 minutes before serving. Half fill fondue saucepot with oil; heat until oil is gently bubbling. Spear meat with fondue forks. Cook until desired doneness (about 1 minute). Transfer meat to plate; dip into a choice of sauces. 4 servings.

Sauces:

For each sauce, mix ingredients listed in small serving dishes (about ½ cup size).

Curry Sauce:

⅓ can condensed cream of celery
   soup (about ⅓ cup)

2 tablespoons mayonnaise
1 teaspoon curry powder

Serve with dishes of toasted coconut and chopped chutney.

Mock Bearnaise Sauce:

⅓ can condensed cream of celery
   soup (about ⅓ cup)

2 tablespoons mayonnaise
1 tablespoon tarragon vinegar
1 teaspoon chervil, crushed

Horseradish Sauce:

⅓ can condensed cream of celery
   soup (about ⅓ cup)

2 tablespoons sour cream
1 tablespoon horseradish

Serve with a small dish of finely chopped green onion.

Italian Trattoria Buffet

Serve this delightful menu buffet-style to guests who will sit at small tables, covered with informal cloths and colorful appointments in the style of an Italian trattoria, rustic restaurant. To make the antipasti salad, arrange on a bed of greens a variety of olives, sardines, tuna, artichoke hearts, pickled peppers, salami slices, hard-cooked egg wedges and marinated mushrooms. Prepare beforehand and chill. The manicotti can be partly prepared ahead of time and baked after the guests arrive. Serve chianti wine with dinner, and make Espresso for a grand finale.

Minestrone au Pistou

1 medium clove garlic, minced
1 teaspoon basil, crushed
2 tablespoons Parmesan cheese
1 teaspoon tomato paste

1 tablespoon olive oil
2 cans (10¾ ounces each)
  condensed minestrone soup
2 soup cans water

Using a bowl and wooden spoon (or a mortar and pestle), pound garlic and basil into a paste. Blend in cheese and tomato paste. Add oil. In saucepan, heat soup and water. Stir garlic mixture into soup. Serve with additional cheese. 4 to 6 servings.

Manicotti

8 manicotti (about ¼ pound)
  macaroni
2 cups (1 pound) dry cottage
  cheese
1 egg, slightly beaten
⅓ cup grated Parmesan cheese
¼ cup finely chopped parsley
½ pound ground beef
⅓ cup chopped onion

2 medium cloves garlic, minced
1 teaspoon basil, crushed
1 teaspoon oregano, crushed
2 cans (10¾ ounces each)
  condensed tomato soup
½ cup water
2 slices (3 ounces) Mozzarella
  cheese, cut into 8 triangles

Cook manicotti until tender; drain. Combine cottage cheese, egg, Parmesan, and parsley; fill manicotti. Arrange manicotti in shallow baking dish (12x8x2 inches). In saucepan, brown meat and cook onion, garlic, basil, and oregano until onion is tender. Stir in soup and water. Pour over manicotti. Bake at 350° F. for 35 minutes. Top with Mozzarella. Bake until cheese melts. 4 servings.

An Italian Trattoria Buffet is a fun and informal party featuring Manicotti *and Antipasti Salad.*

Royal Hawaiian Luau

Punch Bowl and Pupus
Rumaki*
Turban of Flounder,
Macadamia*
Snow Peas or Sweet Peas
Spinach Salad Bowl
Cheese Cake
Iced Coffee or Tea

Transport your guests to the charming informality of Hawaii with this appealing menu. The entertaining area can become a tropical garden with greenery, potted plants and fresh flowers. Use colorful lanterns. Decorate the table with green leaves and a centerpiece of fresh fruit (including pineapples). Ask everyone to come in island costume—slacks and bright aloha shirts for men, and mumuus for the women. Give paper or flower leis to each guest. Don't forget lyrical Hawaiian music. Allow sufficient time to make the delectable main dish and Rumaki.

Rumaki

1 package (8 ounces) frozen
  chicken livers
3 tablespoons soy sauce

Dash ginger
1 tablespoon sugar
6 water chestnuts, quartered
8 slices bacon, cut in thirds

Thaw livers as directed on package; cut into 24 pieces. Combine soy, ginger, and sugar; marinate livers in mixture for 30 minutes at room temperature. Drain. Fold a piece of liver over water chestnut. Wrap bacon around liver; fasten with toothpick. Bake in pan on rack at 350°F. for 35 minutes or until bacon is crisp. Makes 24 appetizers.

Turban of Flounder, Macadamia

1 cup sliced celery
3 tablespoons butter or margarine
2 cans (10½ ounces each)
  condensed chicken broth
⅓ cup raw regular rice
2 cups diced cooked shrimp
½ cup drained pineapple tidbits

8 thin flounder fillets (about 2
  pounds)
¼ cup sliced green onion
2 tablespoons Sherry
¼ cup chopped Macadamia nuts
1 tablespoon chopped pimiento
2 tablespoons cornstarch

In saucepan, cook celery in 2 tablespoons butter until tender. Add ¾ cup broth and the rice. Bring to a boil. Cover; cook over low heat 20 minutes or until all liquid is absorbed. Add shrimp and pineapple. Line a 5-cup well-buttered ring mold with fish as follows: alternating wide and narrow ends, overlap fillets, and let ends hang over outside of mold; fill with shrimp mixture; fold fillet ends over top; place mold on baking sheet. Bake at 350° F. for 40 minutes. To pour off excess liquid, place cake rack over mold; invert but do not unmold. Unmold on serving platter. Meanwhile, in saucepan, cook onion in 1 tablespoon butter. Add 1 can broth, Sherry, nuts, and pimiento. Combine cornstarch with remaining broth (½ cup); stir into sauce. Cook, stirring until thickened. Serve over mold. 8 servings.

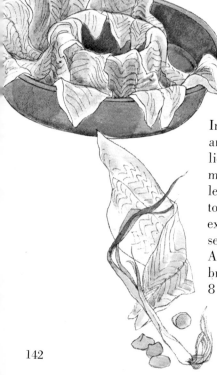

Parisian Dinner Menu

When dining in gay Paree, you may sample elegant and complicated dishes amid regal surroundings or enjoy the pleasantries of robust country fare in an informal bistro. No matter the setting, the food will be honest and good, prepared with care and devotion. Your friends will be enchanted with this delightful dinner, planned with continental flair. For a French touch to frozen peas, add a little chopped lettuce, butter, pinch of sugar, salt and pepper to them while cooking. Chilled white wine may be served with the dinner. Prepare the chocolate souffle early in the day and refrigerate; for a midnight garnish, top with puffs of whipped cream plus tiny stars and a crescent moon cut from thin orange rind.

Liver Pate* or
French Onion Soup*
(see index)

Chicken Magnifique with
White and Wild Rice*
or Chicken in
Champagne Sauce*

French Peas

Croissants

Cold Chocolate

Midnight Souffle

Demitasse

❇ *Chicken Magnifique*

4 whole chicken breasts (about
  3 pounds), split
¼ cup butter or margarine
2 cups sliced mushrooms (about
  ½ pound)
2 cans (10½ ounces each)
  condensed cream of chicken
  soup

1 large clove garlic, minced
Generous dash crushed thyme
⅛ teaspoon rosemary, crushed
⅔ cup light cream
2 packages (6 ounces each)
  long grain and wild rice mix,
  prepared

Use 1 large skillet or prepare in 2 skillets (10 inch) by dividing the ingredients equally. Brown chicken in butter; remove. Brown mushrooms. Stir in soup, garlic, and seasonings; add chicken. Cover; cook over low heat 30 minutes or until chicken is tender. Stir now and then. Blend in cream; heat slowly. Serve with rice. 8 servings.

Wine: Add ½ cup Sauterne or Sherry with soup. Decrease light cream to ½ cup.

Chicken in Champagne Sauce

5 whole chicken breasts (about
  4 pounds), split, skinned,
  and boned
¼ cup butter or margarine
1 split (8 ounces) Champagne

1 can (10½ ounces) condensed
  cream of chicken soup
1 can (10½ ounces) condensed
  cream of mushroom soup
⅓ cup light cream
Chopped parsley

In skillet, lightly brown chicken in butter (about 5 minutes each side); remove. Add Champagne to skillet, stirring to loosen browned bits and cooking until ½ the original volume. Stir in soups and cream; add chicken. Cook over low heat 20 minutes. Stir now and then. Garnish with parsley. 8 to 10 servings.

143

Spanish Summertime Buffet

The Spanish love to dine outdoors amid a gay and colorful atmosphere. Capture the true Spanish spirit for a lovely buffet party with vibrant colors such as red and black. Wrought iron items can be used. Serve the cold Gazpacho soup-salad in parfait glasses, cups, or bowls before the meal; the garnishes of chopped vegetables and croutons add to the delight of this dish. For the salad, slice large mild onions and oranges and sprinkle with oil and lemon juice. Prepare the custard in one large dish or smaller individual ones. Lively guitar or flamenco music in the background will add to the atmosphere.

✳ *Gazpacho*

2 medium cloves garlic, minced
2 tablespoons olive oil
3 cans (10¾ ounces each)
condensed tomato soup
3 cups cold water

¼ cup wine vinegar
2 cups chopped cucumber
1 cup chopped green pepper
½ cup chopped onion
Croutons

In small saucepan, cook garlic in olive oil; combine in a large bowl with soup, water, and vinegar. Chill for 4 hours. Serve in chilled bowls. Pass chilled vegetables and croutons for garnish. 6 to 9 servings.

Blender Version: Cook garlic as above. Combine in electric blender with 1 can soup, 1 cup water, ¼ cup cucumber, ¼ cup green pepper, 2 tablespoons onion, and 2 slices toast. Blend until smooth; combine in a large bowl with remaining soup, water, and vinegar. Chill as above. Garnish with remaining vegetables.

✳ *Spanish Paella*

3 pounds chicken parts
4 tablespoons salad oil
1 can (10¾ ounces) condensed
tomato soup
1 can (10½ ounces) condensed
onion soup
2½ soup cans water
4 medium cloves garlic, minced
2 teaspoons oregano, crushed

2 teaspoons salt
⅛ teaspoon pepper
2 pounds raw shrimp, cleaned
and deveined
2 cups raw regular rice
2 large green peppers, cut in
strips
1 cup chopped pimiento
⅔ cup sliced ripe olives

Use 1 large skillet or prepare in 2 skillets (about 10 inch), by dividing ingredients equally. Brown chicken in oil; pour off fat. Stir in soups, water, garlic, and seasonings. Cover; cook over low heat 15 minutes. Stir in remaining ingredients. Cover; cook over low heat 30 minutes or until chicken and rice are tender. Stir now and then. 8 to 10 servings.

For an occasion your guests will never forget, arrange a Spanish Summertime Buffet with cold Gazpacho soup and a sumptuous Paella.

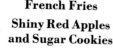

Winter Get-Together

After a vigorous skating session or hike in the snow, gather the group at your house for warming fare. This menu can be ready in minutes if the Souperburgers are prepared partially beforehand. Serve the soup in mugs. Arrange the other food on a buffet where guests can help themselves. Double or triple soups as needed.

Peanut Soup

¼ cup finely chopped celery
¼ cup finely chopped onion
2 tablespoons butter or margarine
1 can (10½ ounces)
condensed cream of
chicken soup

⅓ cup peanut butter
1 soup can milk
Chopped peanuts

In saucepan, cook celery and onion in butter until tender. Blend in soup and peanut butter until smooth. Add milk. Heat; stir now and then. Garnish with peanuts. 2 to 3 servings.

Oyster Chowder

1 can (10¼ ounces) condensed
oyster stew
1 soup can milk
1 cup cubed cooked potatoes

½ cup diced cooked ham
1 tablespoon chopped parsley
⅛ teaspoon leaf thyme

In saucepan, combine all ingredients. Heat; stir now and then. 2 to 3 servings.

❋ Souperburger

1 pound ground beef
½ cup chopped onion
1 tablespoon shortening
1 can (10½ ounces) condensed
chicken gumbo, golden
mushroom, tomato,
vegetable, or cream of
mushroom soup

1 tablespoon prepared mustard
Dash pepper
6 buns, split and toasted

In skillet, brown beef and cook onion in shortening until tender; stir to separate meat. Pour off fat. Add soup and seasonings. Cook 5 minutes; stir now and then. Serve on buns. Makes 6 sandwiches.

Impromptu Supper

When you invite neighbors on the spur of the moment for a celebration or a gathering for newcomers, it helps to have some pantry-shelf specials to bring out. The menu should be easy to prepare but delectable. This one is. The dessert comes from the freezer—today's frozen layer cakes are a boon to the hurried hostess. Double or triple soups as needed.

Many Way Chowder,*

Soup Mediterranean*
or Chili Soup*

**Platter of Cheeses,
Sliced Tomatoes, Pickles,
and Hard-Cooked Eggs**

Assorted Hot Breads

Butter

**Chocolate or
Coconut Layer Cake**

Coffee

❈ *Many Way Chowder*

¼ cup sliced celery
2 tablespoons chopped onion
1 tablespoon butter or margarine
1 can (10½ ounces) condensed
  cream of mushroom or
  potato soup
½ soup can milk
½ soup can water

1 cup cubed cooked chicken or
  ham; or 1 can (7 ounces)
  minced clams or tuna,
  drained
½ cup cooked cut green beans,
  mixed vegetables, peas, or
  chopped canned tomatoes

In saucepan, cook celery and onion in butter until tender. Stir in soup; gradually blend in milk and water. Add remaining ingredients. Heat; stir now and then. 2 to 3 servings.

Soup Mediterranean

1 can (2 ounces) sliced mush-
  rooms, drained
Generous dash crushed oregano
1 tablespoon butter or margarine

1 can (10¾ ounces) condensed
  minestrone soup
1 soup can water
½ cup cubed cooked beef,
  chicken, lamb, or pork

In saucepan, brown mushrooms with oregano in butter. Add remaining ingredients. Heat; stir now and then. 2 to 3 servings.

❈ *Chili Soup*

1 pound ground beef
½ cup chopped green pepper
½ cup chopped onion
1 teaspoon chili powder

2 cans (11 ounces each) condensed
  chili beef soup
1½ soup cans water
1 cup chopped canned tomatoes

In large saucepan, brown beef and cook green pepper and onion with chili powder until tender. Stir in remaining ingredients. Heat; stir now and then. 4 to 6 servings.

Convenient Casserole Dinner

This is a dinner for casual entertaining. Guests will enjoy the Frisky Sours, a refreshing combination of beef broth and lemon juice. Bake the casserole in an attractive dish which can be brought to the table. Such a hearty casserole and big salad are a favorite menu for many a hostess and for guests. Make the cake "from-scratch" or start with a spice cake mix. This famous surprise cake (made with tomato soup as the liquid) has intrigued and pleased homemakers for more than 40 years.

Frisky Sours
Recipe may be doubled

1 can (10½ ounces) condensed
beef broth
½ cup water

2 tablespoons lemon juice
6 ice cubes

Place all ingredients in a shaker; cover and shake well. Serve garnished with lemon twists. 3 servings.

Cracked Ice: Omit water and ice cubes; substitute 1½ soup cans cracked ice.

Company Veal Casserole

2 pounds veal cutlet
(about ½ inch thick)
Salt and pepper
½ cup chopped onion
2 large cloves garlic, minced
¼ cup butter or margarine
1 can (10¾ ounces) condensed
Cheddar cheese soup
1 can (10½ ounces) condensed
cream of mushroom soup

⅔ cup milk
¼ cup Sauterne or other
dry white wine
¼ cup chopped pimiento
3 cups cooked wide noodles
(5 to 6 ounces uncooked)
2 packages (9 ounces each)
Italian green beans,
cooked and drained

Pound veal with meat hammer or edge of heavy saucer; sprinkle with salt and pepper. Cut into 1-inch pieces. In skillet, brown veal and cook onion with garlic in butter until tender. In 3-quart casserole, stir soups until smooth; gradually blend in milk, wine, and pimiento. Stir in veal mixture, noodles, and green beans. Bake at 350° F. for 40 minutes or until hot. 6 to 8 servings.

❋ Tomato Spice Cake

Pictured on back cover

2¼ cups cake flour or 2
   cups all-purpose flour
1⅓ cups sugar
4 teaspoons baking powder
1 teaspoon baking soda
1½ teaspoons allspice
1 teaspoon cinnamon

½ teaspoon ground cloves
1 can (10¾ ounces)
   condensed tomato soup
½ cup hydrogenated shortening
2 eggs
¼ cup water

Preheat oven to 350° F. Generously grease and flour 2 round layer pans, 8 or 9 inches, or an oblong pan, 13 x 9 x 2 inches. Measure dry ingredients into large bowl. Add soup and shortening. Beat at low to medium speed for 2 minutes (300 strokes with a spoon) scraping sides and bottom of bowl constantly. Add eggs and water. Beat 2 minutes more, scraping bowl frequently. Pour into pans. Bake 35 to 40 minutes. Let stand in pans 10 minutes; remove and cool on rack. Frost with *Cream Cheese Frosting.*

Bundt Pan: Proceed as above. Bake in well-greased and lightly floured 2½-quart bundt pan at 350° F. for 50 to 60 minutes or until done. Cool right side up in pan 15 minutes; remove from pan. Cool. If desired, sprinkle cake with confectioners' sugar.

❋ Quick Tomato Spice Cake

1 package (2 layer) spice cake mix
1 can (10¾ ounces) condensed
   tomato soup

½ cup water
2 eggs

Mix *only* above ingredients, following directions on package. If desired, fold in 1 cup chopped walnuts. Bake as directed. Frost with *Cream Cheese Frosting* or other favorite white frosting.

Cream Cheese Frosting

2 packages (3 ounces each)
   cream cheese, softened
1 package (1 pound) sifted
   confectioners' sugar

½ teaspoon vanilla extract,
   optional

Blend cream cheese until smooth. Gradually blend in sugar and vanilla. If necessary, thin with milk. Makes enough frosting for two 8 or 9-inch layers.

TUREEN SUPPER

Tickets for the theater or a pops-concert call for a most special little supper—either before or after the fact. Famous hostesses have set a style for supper planned around a beautiful tureen of soup. Here's the chance to show off the heirloom soup container from Grandmother—with extra-special food. The tureen shown is a famous George III silver design of 1810 by Paul Storr who was a royal silversmith in England. Double or triple soups as needed.

Bisque a la Crab* or
Chicken Soup New Orleans*
Romaine, Avocado,
and Grapefruit Salad
Hot Popovers
Raspberry Parfait
Nuts   Mints
Demitasse

❊Bisque A La Crab

½ cup diagonally sliced celery
¼ teaspoon chervil, crushed
2 tablespoons butter or margarine
1 can (10¾ ounces) condensed
    Cheddar cheese soup
1 can (10½ ounces) condensed
    cream of chicken soup

1½ soup cans milk
¼ cup Sherry
2 packages (6 ounces each) frozen
    crab, thawed and drained
    (1½ cups)
⅓ cup sliced water chestnuts

In saucepan, cook celery with chervil in butter until tender. Stir in remaining ingredients. Heat; stir now and then. 4 servings.

Lobster: Substitute 1½ cups cubed cooked lobster for crab.

Chicken Soup New Orleans

1 cup diced cooked ham
½ cup chopped onion
⅛ teaspoon leaf thyme, crushed
Generous dash poultry seasoning
1 tablespoon butter or margarine
3 cans (10½ ounces each) con-
    densed chicken gumbo soup

3 soup cans water
1 cup cubed cooked chicken
1 package (10 ounces) frozen
    asparagus cuts, cooked
    and drained

In large pan, lightly brown ham and cook onion with thyme and poultry seasoning in butter until tender. Add remaining ingredients. Heat; stir now and then. 6 servings.

Weekend Patio Party

This relaxing menu features one dish to be cooked on a rotisserie or grill out-of-doors. For the salad combine cold cooked rice, diced onion, sliced stuffed olives and celery with a tangy salad dressing. Chill. Make the biscuit shortcakes before-hand and serve two or three fruits such as strawberries, raspberries, and honeydew melon cubes for guests to make their own desserts. Cover the table with a pastel paper or cotton cloth and use pretty candles in hurricane lamps.

❊ *Soup-On-The-Rocks*

The easiest and most popular of frosted soups is yours to enjoy anywhere. Simply fill a broad glass with ice cubes. Pour beef broth, right from the can, over the cubes. Garnish with a slice or wedge of lemon or lime.

Note: For variety add a fleck of spice to the beef broth before pouring over ice cubes, perhaps curry, nutmeg, cinnamon, allspice, or ginger.

❊ *Garden Asparagus Soup*
Recipe may be doubled

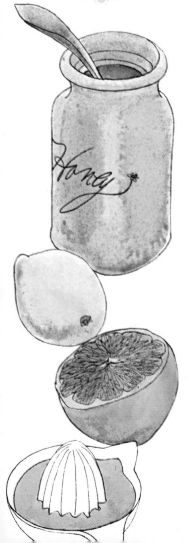

*1 can (10½ ounces) condensed
    cream of asparagus soup*
½ cup sour cream

½ soup can water
½ teaspoon dried dill leaves, crushed
Chopped cucumber or watercress

In saucepan, blend soup and sour cream; add water and dill. Heat; stir now and then. Garnish with cucumber. 2 to 3 servings.

Chilled Version: Increase water to 1 cup. Combine all ingredients; chill.

Cornish Hens with Orange-Honey Sauce

*2 cans (10½ ounces each)
    condensed chicken broth*
⅔ cup orange sections cut-up
½ cup orange juice

⅓ cup honey
¼ cup cornstarch
2 tablespoons lemon juice
½ teaspoon grated orange rind

In saucepan, combine all ingredients. Cook over low heat, stirring until thickened. Makes 3½ cups sauce.

Rock Cornish Hens *(Outdoor Method):* Truss 4 Rock Cornish Hens (about 1½ pounds each). Mount and balance hens close together and tie on spit. Place on rotisserie over glowing coals. Place drip pan under hens. Cook 45 minutes. Meanwhile, prepare sauce. Cook 45 minutes more or until tender, brushing frequently with sauce. Heat remaining sauce; serve with hens. 4 to 6 servings.

Rock Cornish Hens *(Indoor Method):* Roast 4 Rock Cornish Hens (about 1½ pounds each) at 400°F. for 45 minutes. Meanwhile, prepare sauce. Bake hens 30 minutes more or until tender, brushing frequently with sauce. Heat remaining sauce; serve with hens. 4 to 6 servings.

Provencal Picnic For Couples

Prepare a picnic for an outdoor get-together which features delectable dishes of Provence, that beautiful and romantic Mediterranean region of France. Robust and hearty, well flavored with garlic and herbs, the native fare is colorful and appealing. The soup will need to go in a big wide-mouth thermos or jug to keep hot.

❋ *Puree Mongole*

*1 can (11¼ ounces) condensed
   green pea soup
1 can (10¾ ounces) condensed
   tomato soup*

*1 cup milk
1 cup water
Dash curry powder, optional*

In saucepan, stir green pea soup until smooth; gradually blend in remaining ingredients. Heat; stir now and then. Do not boil. 4 to 5 servings.

Beef Soup Riviera
Recipe may be doubled

*¼ cup sliced green onion
2 tablespoons butter or margarine
1 can (10¾ ounces) condensed
   beef soup*

*1 cup water
¼ cup orange juice
2 tablespoons toasted slivered almonds
2 orange slices, quartered*

In saucepan, cook onion in butter until tender. Add soup, water, orange juice, and almonds. Heat; stir now and then. Garnish with orange. 2 to 3 servings.

Salad Nicoise

Dressing:

*1 can (10¾ ounces) condensed
   tomato soup
½ cup salad oil
¼ cup wine vinegar
2 tablespoons sugar
1 tablespoon minced onion
2 teaspoons dry mustard
1 teaspoon salt
¼ teaspoon pepper*

Salad Ingredients:

*4 cups sliced cooked potatoes
1 package (9 ounces) frozen cut
   green beans, cooked
   and drained
Salad greens
1 can (7 ounces) tuna, drained
1 medium tomato cut in wedges
2 hard-cooked eggs, quartered
Ripe olives
Anchovy fillets*

Combine soup, oil, vinegar, sugar, onion, mustard, salt, and pepper in a tightly covered container. Shake well. Mix potatoes with ¾ cup dressing and green beans with ¼ cup dressing. Chill all ingredients. On a large platter place salad greens. Arrange potatoes, green beans, and tuna; garnish with remaining ingredients. Serve with additional dressing. 4 servings.

TEEN-AGERS' DANCING PARTY

Teen-agers will line up in a hurry to partake of this buffet with an Italian theme. For the fresh fruit kabobs, arrange alternately pineapple cubes, berries, red grapes, cubes of apple or peaches on small skewers and chill.

❋ *Meat-za Pizza*

*1 can (10¾ ounces) condensed
   tomato or Cheddar cheese
   soup**
1½ pounds ground beef
½ cup fine dry bread crumbs
¼ cup minced onion

1 egg, slightly beaten
1 teaspoon salt
1 medium clove garlic, minced
⅛ teaspoon oregano, crushed
*3 ounces Mozzarella or
   mild process cheese, sliced*

Mix thoroughly ½ cup soup with all ingredients except cheese; pat meat evenly on baking sheet into 10-inch circle with 1-inch stand-up rim. Or use a cookie sheet placing a 16-inch long sheet of aluminum foil (double thickness or heavy duty) on it, turning up edges and sealing corners to hold drippings. Bake at 450° F. for 10 minutes. Spoon off fat. Spread rest of soup on meat; top with cheese. Sprinkle with additional oregano. Top with mushrooms, anchovies, olives, or sausage, if desired. Bake 10 minutes more. Cut into wedges and serve. 6 servings.

*If using Cheddar cheese soup, substitute 4 slices tomato, cut in quarters for sliced cheese.

❋ *Coney Islands*

Recipe may be doubled

4 frankfurters, split lengthwise
1 tablespoon butter or margarine
*1 can (11 ounces) condensed
   chili beef soup*

⅓ cup water
*4 frankfurter rolls, split
   and toasted*
Chopped onion

In skillet, brown frankfurters in butter. Add soup and water. Heat, stirring now and then. Place frankfurters in rolls; spoon chili over. Top with onions. Garnish with shredded mild process cheese, sliced stuffed olives, chopped green pepper, or sliced pickles. Makes 4 sandwiches.

Meat-za Pizza and Coney Islands will attract all Teenagers who love to gather for hearty food after the big dance.

INDEX